Supply Chain Logistics
Foundational Knowledge
For Frontline Workers

**Leo Reddy
and
Rebekah Hutton**

This product was funded by a grant awarded under the President's High Growth Job Training Initiative as implemented by the U.S. Department of Labor's Employment & Training Administration. The information contained in this product was created by a grantee organization and does not necessarily reflect the official position of the U.S. Department of Labor. All references to non-governmental companies or organizations, their services, products, or resources are offered for informational purposes and should not be construed as an endorsement by the Department of Labor. This product is copyrighted by the institution that created it and is intended for individual organizational, non-commercial use only.

Copyright © 2013 by Manufacturing Skill Standards Council

All rights reserved. Except as permitted under the United States Copyright Act, no part of this publication may be reproduced or distributed in any form or by any means, or stored in a database or retrieval system, without prior written permission of the publisher, Manufacturing Skill Standards Council.

Send permission requests to:
Manufacturing Skill Standards Council
901 North Washington Street
Suite 600
Alexandria, VA 22314
www.msscusa.org

Supply Chain Logistics

Foreword

Foreword to the Third Edition

This book describes the foundational-level knowledge that frontline workers in supply chain logistics should understand.

To remain competitive, logistics companies increasingly need a flexible, knowledgeable, problem-solving workforce. This means workers who can keep pace with rapid changes in technology and processes, be easily trainable and work in a global environment. These workers must also be competent in the critical work activities common across all facilities within the supply chain: safety, quality control, communications, teamwork, good workplace conduct and key computer systems and equipment that support supply chain operations.

The starting point for defining these core competencies must be industry itself. The the Manufacturing Skill Standards Council (MSSC), has been a national leader since 1998 in developing industry-led skill standards for the foundational knowledge of front-line workers. Once the standards are established, MSSC assesses workforce skills against those standards and issues an industry-recognized, nationally portable certificate to individuals who pass the certification assessments.

In 2008, logistics industry subject matter experts identified skills standards for two levels of certification. The first is the Certified Logistics Associate (CLA), based upon the individual's command of the foundational knowledge and skills described in this textbook. The second is the mid-level Certified Logistics Technician (CLT), based upon the individual's command of the more detailed knowledge and skills described in the companion textbook, _Supply Chain Logistics: Mid-level Technical Knowledge_.

Both CLA and CLT address the work activities and related skills involved with moving material throughout the supply chain: to and from production sites, to warehouses and distribution centers, to material handlers within the various transportation modes. They do not, however, address the specific skills involved in actually operating vehicles within those transportation modes or operating material handling equipment.

This book and its companion, _Supply Chain Logistics: Mid-level Technical Knowledge_, are aligned with MSSC standards for CLA and CLT and help individuals learn topics covered by those standards and the related certification assessments. However, these books should be viewed as primers for their respective levels. One of their purposes is to generate interest and further education in this field, so that workers will continuously enhance their knowledge and improve the performance of their companies.

Teachers and students are thus encouraged to use other books in this field as a companion to this one. A bibliography is included for that purpose and provides a sample of some of the leading sources of expertise. In addition, teachers and students are encouraged to use complementary materials and courses, including hands-on courses and on-the-job training that help individuals improve their knowledge and skills.

Supply Chain Logistics

Forward

It is not MSSC policy to require individuals to take any preparatory course or provide documentation of experience prior to taking the CLA or CLT assessments required for certification. Those assessments are delivered at MSSC authorized testing sites. Anyone wishing to know the location of those sites or interested in establishing a site should refer to the points of contact on the MSSC Web Site (www.msscusa.org).

MSSC hopes that individuals and stakeholder organizations will make active use of this textbook and related education and training resources. The foundational knowledge and skills described herein can be used by workers, students, companies, educators and trainers in various settings. MSSC also provides on a fully on-line version of the CLA and CLT courses.

Since the first publication of this primer, two important achievements have occurred:

1. The CLT certification was accredited by the American National Standards Institute (ANSI), under ISO Standard 17024 (personnel certification). This accreditation is noted on the CLT certificate documentation. Employers value ISO and understand the rigor required to earn such a designation.

2. In 2012, the National College Credit Recommendation Service, recommended 4 hours of credit for the combined CLA and CLT courses. Over 1500 colleges and universities nationwide have agreed to consider offering the credits recommended by NCCRS. To learn more about this opportunity and to see if your area college offers credit, visit our website at www.msscusa.org/nccrs.

MSSC and many other parties who participated in writing this book hope that it will lead to the following outcomes:

- Sufficient numbers of individuals within the workforce possessing the skills needed to help companies become more globally competitive, productive and innovative

- A larger pool of CLA-certified workers to reduce company recruiting costs and eliminate expenditures for remedial training

- The widespread use of industry-recognized, nationally portable CLA certificates by workers to credential their knowledge and skills

- A solid foundation for students and workers to build attractive, rewarding careers in the challenging interconnected world of supply chain logistics

- A tool for educators and trainers to provide lively and relevant education and training

- College credit toward continuing education for individuals who have received this training and earned the credential

- A contribution to the prosperity of communities, citizens and companies through the increasingly efficient and cost-effective movement of materials from producer to consumer.

Acknowledgements

The preparation of this primer was supported by a U.S. Department of Labor (USDOL) grant to the North Central Texas Workforce Development Board. Under this grant, the Manufacturing Skill Standards Council (MSSC) was contracted in July 2007 to develop a certification program for front-line workers in supply chain logistics. The Department placed this grant under the "advanced manufacturing" section of its High Growth Jobs Initiative program. MSSC is a national leader in developing standards-based training, assessment and certification programs for the core competencies of front-line industrial workers.

This program is analogous to the one that MSSC has developed since the National Skill Standards Council officially recognized MSSC's industry-led, nationally validated foundational standards for production support workers in 2001. Covering all sectors of manufacturing, this program leads to the well-established Certified Production Technician (CPT) certification.

As with CPT, the CLT certification program for supply chain logistics includes standards, assessments and credentials, supported by courses, textbooks, teacher certification training, a registry and computer-based learning technologies.

The CLT certification program was publicly announced at a special event, "Training and Certifying the Workforce of the Future," at the ProMat 2009 International Logistics Show in Chicago on January 14, 2009, supported by the Material Handling Industry of America (MHIA). Under the USDOL grant, teachers will be trained in the North Texas area in February and March, 2009, with courses beginning for 250 trainees in April, 2009. A North Texas Advanced Manufacturing and Logistics Summit in Dallas, in March 2009, inaugurated this training and outreach to the logistics community in that large intermodal hub.

The preparation of this primer, Supply Chain Logistics: Foundational Knowledge, was a team effort in every way. The MSSC would first like to thank the U.S. Department of Labor's Employment and Training Administration for funding the development of the CLT program and the grant project team, led by Kent Andersen, Natalie Johnson and Marcia Brown at the North Central Texas Workforce Development Board, and Drew Casani and Rick Askew at the Texas Manufacturing Assistance Center. Steve Boecking, Vice President, Hillwood Alliance Global Logistics Hub in Fort Worth, played a key role in recruiting the industry subject matter experts who wrote the initial CLT standards.

This text is organized and formatted around the industry-led standards for CLA. It is largely a compilation of materials written by leading authorities in this field aligned with the content of those standards. Leo Reddy and Rebekah Hutton at MSSC conducted the research, prepared the initial drafts for expert review and edited the text. John Rauschenberger, Ph.D., edited the third edition.

Supply Chain Logistics

Acknowledgements

Ruben Johnson, Dean of Business at Cedar Valley College in the Dallas Country Community College District and a former Marine Corps supply officer, made useful suggestions for source documents. Theresa Chin Jones and Dave Jones of Pro-Writers assisted with some of the initial drafting. MSSC owes special thanks to two leading industry experts for the first line of review of the initial drafts: Bob Nichol and Phil Carlson, former logistics directors from Best Buy and Kraft Foods, respectively. Athleen Reddy edited the text at each stage of drafting and review.

We want to acknowledge the critical role played by Allan Howie, Director of Continuing Education and Professional Development at the Material Handling Industry of America (MHIA). Allan provided guidance on curriculum development from the beginning, was one of the key reviewers and served as a principal organizer of the Special Event at the Pro Mat 2009 International Logistics Show. In addition, Allan's own landmark work, Fundamentals of Warehousing and Distribution, An Introductory Course in Material Handling, was the single most important source document for this primer.

Many other individuals reviewed this text and provided expert feedback.
These are:

Lloyd Clive, Fleming College; Sherman Johnson, Ivy Tech Community College of Indiana; Dave Rubright, Lehigh Career & Technical Institute; Mike Stroh, the Logistics Network; Michael Johl; and Angela Traiforos, J. W. Reed, Sam Deckich and Cory Lane of Community Learning Center, Inc.

In addition, we want to express thanks to the several authors of recent textbooks in this field, whose advanced thinking and practical guidance formed the critical source of authoritative expertise. They are referenced in the text and identified in the Bibliography.

Supply Chain Logistics

Table of Contents

Welcome to the Reader 8

Chapter 1 13
Global Supply Chain Logistics

Chapter 2 25
The Logistics Environment

Chapter 3 37
Material Handling Equipment

Chapter 4 51
Safety Principles

Chapter 5 63
Safe Material Handling & Equipment Operation

Chapter 6 75
Quality Control Principles

Chapter 7 87
Work Communication

Chapter 8 93
Teamwork & Good Workplace Conduct to Solve Problems

Chapter 9 107
Using Computers

Glossary of Terms 114

Notes 117

Bilbliography 118

Supply Chain Logistics

Welcome

Welcome to the Reader

Welcome to the world of global supply chain logistics!

As noted at the beginning of Chapter 1, supply chain logistics is "the lifeblood of the world economy." It is the flow of material, information and money from the producer to the consumer. You are familiar with the products that we all use in our daily lives, but those products have no value to the manufacturer or the consumer unless they can be delivered in a safe and timely manner.

This book focuses on the material handling portion of global supply chain logistics. It describes the foundational knowledge that frontline material handling workers should master to perform well. Most of you who gain this knowledge can look forward to a rewarding career. These careers provide good wages and benefits and a clear pathway to higher levels of skills and responsibility.

Global supply chain logistics, a modern concept, also embodies the evolution of logistics as one of the earliest activities of mankind with a profound influence on course of history.

Let us briefly review that history, its expression in the modern economy and the rewarding careers offered in the field of supply chain logistics today.

A Military Legacy

What is the first thing you think about when you hear the word "logistics"?

If you answer, "something to do with the military" you would not be far off. The term itself has its roots in military history. It comes from the French "marechal de logis," a top general in the army of King Louis XVI responsible for providing lodging, food and supplies to the troops. As recently as 1960, the Oxford Universal Dictionary defined logistics as, "the art of moving and quartering troops".

In military terms, logistics is an organized process of providing all the material needed by war-fighters on the frontlines of combat. This process has a history dating well before the armies of 18th Century King Louis. For example:

- The mythical campaign by Greek states in the 12th Century BC that "launched a thousand ships" to rescue the beautiful Helen of Troy.

- The challenge of provisioning the armies of the Macedonian king, Alexander the Great (356-323 BC), whose conquests extended into India.

Supply Chain Logistics

Welcome

- The use of war elephants by Carthaginian commander Hannibal (247-183 BC) to carry supplies from Carthage to Spain, and over the Pyrenees and the Alps to attack Roman armies in northern Italy.
- The massive network of ships and outposts that provisioned the armies of ancient Rome throughout most of Western Europe for five centuries.

In a more contemporary setting, think of:

- The inability of Napoleon to protect his forces from bitter cold in his retreat from Russia in 1812, during which his army of 500,000 men was reduced to 20,000.
- The treacherous movement of cannon from Lake Champlain to Boston in 1776, where General Washington used them to defeat British forces in Dorchester. [1]
- The accelerated construction of rail roads and canals by President Lincoln's generals to leverage the North's advantage in the production of war material.
- The rapid building of "Victory Ships" by the U.S., the "arsenal of democracy," to provision American and Allied forces during World War II, including the armada of supply ships assembled for D-Day.

Business Logistics

In the second half of the 20th Century, the business community began to use the tools of military logistics within their operations. While the study of traffic management and physical distribution began in the 1950s, increased use of business logistics became popular only in the 1980s. There were several reasons for this:

- Reduction in Regulation – Reductions in economic regulation in the U.S. trucking, airfreight and railroad industries in the 1970s and 1980s allowed individual carriers flexibility in pricing and service.
- Changes in Consumer Behavior – Rising customer expectations for rapid delivery of goods and mass customization compressed timetables for both production and assembly.
- Growing Power of Retailers – Another influence was the emergence of "power retailers," such as Wal-Mart, Best Buy and Home Depot that demanded rapid delivery of products at low cost.
- Just-in-time – In response to sharpening global competitiveness, manufacturers required "just-in-time" delivery of parts and components in order to maintain leaner inventories, speed up delivery and lower warehousing costs.
- Globalization of Trade – The rapid growth of world trade created new challenges, costs and complexities for logistics.[2] Companies are sourcing from more countries, adding new carriers, forwarders, logistics and distribution partners.

Supply Chain Logistics

Welcome

- Rising Costs – The cost of logistics rose by nearly $100 billion to $1.4 trillion in 2007, a record high for the fourth consecutive year and about 10 percent of the U.S. gross domestic product.[3]

- Impact on Corporations – Most U.S. corporations now spend between 8 and 15 percent of sales revenue on logistics activities.[4]

- Technological Advances – Improvements in technology, especially communication technology, have given companies the ability to share information accurately and quickly on a global scale.

- ISO Standardization – The increased use of standardized containers and equipment internationally has improved speed and reliability.

These trends have caused a sharp increase in recent decades in departments within companies that are responsible for the flow of material, information and money throughout the supply chain. They strategically manage the procurement, movement and storage of materials, parts and finished inventory (and the related information flow) through the organization and its marketing channels in such a way that current and future profitability are maximized through cost-effective fulfillment of orders.[5]

Most companies wishing to minimize total costs and provide a better level of service are moving in the direction of supply chain management.[6] Accompanying this trend is a steady rise in the number and sophistication of consultants and software companies providing expertise in various aspects of supply chain logistics management. Their function is also called "business logistics" or "materials management".

The work of supply chain experts has a significant impact on the work of frontline material handlers. These experts use new management and information tools to bring higher levels of innovation and cost savings to day-to-day operations and inventory control.

Another factor affecting all workers in supply chain logistics is the intensified security environment following the September 11, 2001, terrorist attacks on the World Trade Center and the Pentagon.

In general, supply chain logistics is a field of growing importance, complexity and opportunity for challenging careers.

Careers in Supply Chain Logistics

The growing complexity of supply chain logistics and accelerating customer demands are also transforming the activities of frontline workers. Increasingly, workers are needed with a better understanding of the global supply chain, improved problem solving abilities and basic computer skills. In short, they need to have the agility to become "Industrial Athletes of the Future".

This book is intended to help students and trainees develop the knowledge needed to become that kind of 21st Century frontline worker in supply chain logistics and document that knowledge in the form of a nationally recognized CLA Certificate. With this understanding, you will have the foundation to be readily trainable in diverse functions within supply chain logistics facilities.

As world trade increases, jobs for frontline material handling personnel in the U.S. are projected to increase by almost a quarter of a million positions (from 2004 to 2014), according to the U.S. Bureau of Labor statistics. Many of these jobs pay $12 to $15 an hour, about double the federal minimum wage. Many of these jobs also include a benefits package.[7]

In occupations classified by the U.S. Bureau of Labor Statistics as "material moving," there are over 5.8 million jobs, including the following:

- Frontline supervisors of material handling personnel
- Conveyor operators
- Freight, stock and material movers
- Machine feeders and off bearers
- Packers and packagers
- Tank, car and ship loaders
- Truck and delivery drivers

Think in terms of an entire career pathway in global supply chain logistics. Once you have secured a CLA certificate, you should consider preparing for and taking an assessment for the mid-level technical CLT certification. A CLA certificate is a pre-condition for CLT certification.

You can also build on your experience by taking further academic courses, which increase your qualifications to move to higher positions that typically require an associate or baccalaureate degree. Those courses will help you secure more advanced certifications in this field related supply chain management.

Supply Chain Logistics

Welcome

While salaries differ greatly due to size of business and range of responsibility, we will attempt to give you some idea of potential income. Some typical examples of higher level positions within the logistics arena are:

Examples Only

	Salary Range
Senior VP of Logistics	$200,000 plus
VP of Logistics	$150,000 plus
Director of Distribution	$100,000 plus
Operations Manager	$50,000 plus
Warehouse Supervisor	$35,000 plus

At whatever level in which you work, global supply chain logistics is a rapidly growing and changing field with exciting career possibilities. You will also be participating in an activity of critical importance to the economy.

Supply Chain Logistics

Foundational Knowledge:
For Frontline Workers

Chapter 1:
Global Supply Chain Logistics

Chapter 2:
The Logistics Environment

Chapter 3:
Material Handling Equipment

Chapter 4:
Safety Principles

Chapter 5:
Safe Material Handling & Equipment Operation

Chapter 6:
Quality Control Principles

Chapter 7:
Work Communication

Chapter 8:
Teamwork & Good Workplace Conduct to Solve Problems

Chapter 9:
Using Computers

OVERVIEW OF CHAPTER

The purpose of this chapter is to provide an introduction to the world of logistics and the global supply chain and the role of a frontline material handling worker. Supply chain logistics is the process of getting products from one location to another. This chapter explains the roles of various participants in the supply chain and how they work together to get products from one location to another.

OBJECTIVES

When you have completed this chapter, you will be able to do these things.

1. **Describe** the principal elements of the global supply chain logistics life cycle
2. **Describe** the roles and responsibilities with the supply chain
3. **List** the five modes of transportation
4. **Explain** how material handling affects a company's viability and profitability
5. **Define** basic principles of cost effectiveness throughout the supply chain

Supply Chain Logistics

Chapter 1

Did You Know?

Global Supply Chain

Logistics has a huge impact on the domestic and global economy. Logistics facilitates market exchanges, provides a major source of employment and is a major purchaser of assets and materials. In the process of these activities, organizations in the United States spend nearly $800 billion on logistics each year—up from $678 billion in 1990. That is nearly three times the combined annual revenues of General Motors, IBM, and Proctor & Gamble! Worldwide, more than $1.4 trillion is spent annually on logistics and the amount will grow with the continued expansion of the global marketplace.

Source: "Careers in Logistics", Council of Logistics Management, www.clm1.org

Elements of Global Supply Chain Logistics Life Cycle

Global supply chain logistics is the lifeblood of the world economy. It is the process of material, information and money flowing from the source of supply to the consumer. This process occurs within companies, between companies and between nations. This book focuses on the physical flow of material within the global supply chain. To better understand this complex process we begin with some basic definitions.

Supply Chain

In terms of materials, the supply chain is a network of connected facilities, transportation lanes and information systems. This network procures raw materials, transforms them into intermediate and finished products and distributes them to customers through a physical distribution system.

The facilities within a supply chain network include:

- Raw Material Providers – Mines and farms that extract the raw materials needed to produce a product.[1]

- Production Facilities – Sites that convert raw materials into manufactured products. Those sites range from small shops making a few products and parts to large factories assembling many parts into finished products.

- Warehouses and Distribution Centers – Places where materials are stored for future use or through which materials are passed on to transporters. There are some differences between warehouses and distribution centers. Warehouses usually focus more on storage and inventory. Distribution centers focus more on the movement of finished goods to a transport vehicle. However, these facilities

Chapter 1

Supply Chain Logistics

increasingly perform similar functions, so for the purpose of this course the terms will be used interchangeably.

- Transportation – Material transporters who deliver materials to manufacturers, retailers and consumers through various modes.

Supply Chain Logistics

Logistics is the link between facilities within the supply chain. As stated by one expert, "To borrow a sports analogy, logistics is the game played within the supply chain arena."[2]

In the broadest sense, supply chain logistics involves the efficient, effective forward and reverse flow and storage of goods, services and related information between the point of origin and the point of consumption in order to meet customer requirements.

Material handling logistics, the focus of this book, is "the movement, storage, control and protection of materials and products throughout the process of their manufacture, distribution, consumption and disposal".[3]

Global Supply Chain Logistics

Global logistics is the process of moving materials and information across international boundaries within a global network of connected facilities and transportation modes.

Supply Chain Logistics Life Cycle

One way to look at the flow of materials is to picture a product moving through the global supply chain logistics process from the beginning to the end of that product's life.

The force driving a product through its life cycle is the customer. "Customer demand is the fountainhead for all logistics activities."[4] Customers:

- Pay for the initial product
- Pay for the handling of that product as it flows to each facility in the supply chain
- Are the ultimate consumers of the product

As Figure 1.1 illustrates, the life cycle of material flowing through the supply chain is an integrated, interconnected process. Each facility adds its own value, but many of the tasks involved in physically handling the product as it moves through the logistics process are similar. This is why much of the information contained in this book can be applied to whatever tasks are performed in different facilities within the global logistics supply chain.

Another reason to think in terms of material flow as a life cycle is the new trend towards extending product life. Due to environmental concerns, materials are increasingly recycled, reused or recovered after their use by a consumer.[5]

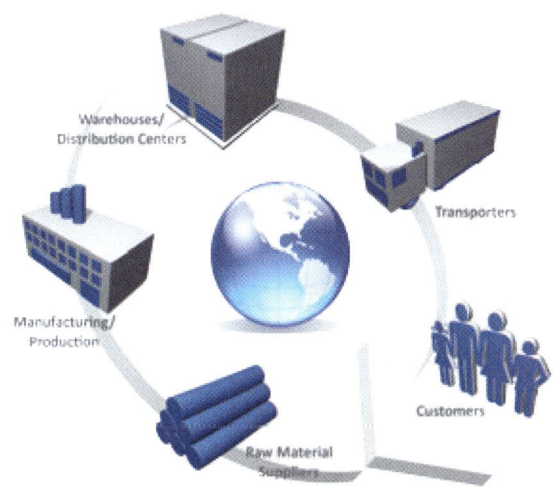

Supply Chain Logistics

Chapter 1

Listerine and the global supply chain

Even a product as simple mouthwash has a supply chain that spans the globe. Consider the following process used to manufacture and sell Listerine mouthwash to consumers in the United States

1. Australian farmers grow eucalyptus, harvest the leaves and send them to a processing company to extract the oil.
2. The eucalyptus oil is then sold to distributors and on to one of Johnson and Johnson's manufacturing plants in Texas.
3. Natural gas is drilled in Saudi Arabia.
4. Union Carbide buys liquid gas and processes it into alcohol, which is shipped to the manufacturing plant in Texas.
5. Farmers in the U.S. Midwest harvest corn.
6. The corn is processed to make Sorbitol which both sweetens and adds bulk to the mouthwash.
7. Sorbitol is sent to the manufacturing plant in Texas.
8. The manufacturing plant collects all of these ingredients and produces the Listerine.
9. The mouthwash is packed and sent to wholesale distributors or directly to retail outlets.

Source: "Listerine website: www.listerine.com, 2008; Kalakota, R. and Robinson, M. (1999) e-Business, roadmap for success, Addison Wesley, Reading, MA

Inventory

Production, warehousing and distribution facilities within the supply chain all contain controlled quantities of materials called inventories. These facilities typically hold inventory in one or more of the following forms:[6]

- Raw materials inventory consisting of materials ready for use in production
- Work-in-Process (WIP) inventory including all the materials currently being processed
- Finished goods inventory of finished products ready for storage or shipment
- In-transit inventory including products that are in the process of being transported from a supplier to a customer

For the most part, this text will discuss inventory as it is controlled through the production facility and as it moves through the rest of the supply chain as a finished product.

Chapter 1

Supply Chain Logistics

Roles and Responsibilities within Supply Chain Logistics

The previous depiction of the global supply chain logistics life cycle simplifies the complex tasks that are carried out at each stage of material handling and movement. To better understand those tasks, it is important to look at the specific roles and responsibilities of each participant in supply chain logistics.

Customer Interaction

The customer drives the supply chain logistics process. A customer can also be a supplier to another customer, so the total chain can have any number of supplier/customer relationships. Customers must specify any special needs including:

- Material handling requirements
- Due dates
- Negotiated terms and conditions
- Acceptance of product substitutions or back orders

Material handlers in the supply chain must be responsive to the customer. They:

- Offer the best value to the customer in terms of cost, quality and delivery

- Control inventory according to the customer's need

- Ensure inventory is available according to customer specifications

- Monitor customer satisfaction

The customer is the driver of the supply chain

Supply Chain Logistics

Chapter 1

Supply

In logistics, supply is the process of sourcing and building product inventory to established targets based on customer needs. The logistics of supply include:

- Identifying and contracting with suppliers of materials
- Working with and integrating multiple sources
- Processing purchase orders
- Verifying timely arrival at the distribution center or warehouse[7]

Warehouses and Distribution Centers

"The roles and responsibilities of warehouses and distribution centers are to minimize the cost of labor, space and equipment, while meeting the timing, shipping and accuracy requirements of the customer."

Most warehousing and distribution centers focus on four basic functions. These are receiving, stocking, order processing and shipping. While each of these areas may have many individual components, they are the core of what makes up most distribution operations.

Receiving

Receiving is more than just the physical receipt of material. It also includes: identifying goods, inspecting for correct quantity and quality using the bill of lading, filling out receiving reports with stock keeping units (SKUs) and quantities, and dispatching the items to the correct location for storage or further distribution. Some, or all, of these activities may be automated. The receiving function is critical because it is the first step in a typical logistics operation. If errors are made in receiving, many of them quite often continue throughout the rest of the material handling chain.

Supply Chain Logistics

Chapter 1

Stocking
Stocking is assigning products to the proper location within the warehouse or distribution center (e.g., rack, bulk or repack) or in some cases directly to a staging area for quick release and shipping. This latter process is sometimes referred to as cross-docking which is becoming more prevalent due to just-in-time inventory techniques.

Order Processing
Order processing is the practice of assembling products from various locations for a specific customer order. It is the basic service a warehouse or distribution center provides for customers and is the function around which most distribution center designs are based.[8]

Picking is the term associated with order processing and can include full case, repack and bulk or pallet picking. As the order is picked from various areas, it is sent to the shipping area for staging.

Packaging is often done in the repack area, if there is one. Full case picks and bulk picks usually have no packaging requirements. However, pallets and other containers are sometimes stretch wrapped for continuity and product protection.

Shipping
Shipping methods are usually determined by the customer. They may include carrier selection, product labeling, palletization or floor loading, product segregation, pallet stretch wrapping, or other terms. Shipping can also include marking, weighing and preparing shipping documents such as, packing slips, address labels and bills of lading.

Loading is the main function of the shipping department. It requires skill and experience to load a trailer, so the product reaches the customer in good condition. The loading or staging area is the last chance to check the load before the customer gets the product. For this reason, it is quite common for auditing of orders to be done at this point. Pallet shipments normally consist of one item per pallet, but in some cases multiple items are combined on a single pallet.

Cross-docking. If goods are brought from elsewhere in the supply chain (e.g., directly from manufacturers or from other warehouses) to fulfill a specific customer order, then they are likely to be cross-docked. This means that the goods are transferred directly from the incoming vehicle to the outgoing vehicle via goods-in and goods-out bays, without being placed into storage. This process is gaining wide acceptance due to inventory carrying cost and the Just-in-Time philosophy of many companies.

To reduce inventory, distribution centers may serve as the final product assembly point. This involves activities such as assembly, testing, cutting and labeling. They may also serve as a returned goods center. This is driven by both environmental legislation and the growth of Internet shopping.[9]

Supply Chain Logistics

Chapter 1

TRUCK

AIR

RAIL

WATER

PIPELINE

Transportation

Transportation physically connects the sources of supply with customers. The role of transportation is to:

- Link all pick-up and deliver-to points
- Meet delivery times specified by the customer
- Deliver via the safest and most cost-effective means
- Dispatch and track vehicles
- Handle products within transportation vehicles according to best practices for safety, security and efficiency
- Meet documentation requirements for state, national and international deliveries
- Handle products in accordance with environmental rules and regulations

Within the supply chain, transportation lanes are used to move inventory between facilities along a particular mode of transportation using a combination of vehicles and containers.[10] The carriers of transportation can be divided into five basic modes: Truck, Air, Rail, Water and Pipeline.

Shared Responsibility

A chain is only as strong as its weakest link. Supply chain logistics is the flow of materials within a network of connected facilities. Each link in the logistics process is dependent on the others. To ensure a strong supply chain, each organization, at every stage in the process, must be aware of this interdependence. It is an important responsibility. Taken together, the work of individuals, beginning with frontline material handlers, impacts on the success or failure of companies within the entire supply chain.

Supply Chain Logistics

Chapter 1

Impact on Company Viability and Profitability

Global supply chain logistics lies at the heart of the viability and profitability of companies within the supply chain. These include companies at all stages: extraction, production, supply, warehousing, distribution and transportation. Effective performance of logistics within the entire supply chain is an increasingly important factor for companies.

Viewing logistics as an integrated system is a relatively recent development. Companies no longer consider logistics in terms of its individual elements (e.g., warehousing, distribution, transportation, etc.). Manufacturers now see logistics as more than a necessary cost of doing business over which they have limited control.

Trends

Economic and global trends have steadily increased the impact of supply chain logistics on companies. These include:

- A sharp rise in global economic competitiveness which puts pressure on companies to reduce costs, enhance quality and increase productivity.

- Widespread adoption of advanced, computer-based technologies which make it possible to gather more information on all company operations.

- The surge in global logistics flows due to the growth in international trade and global access to the Internet for business transactions.

- Growing transportation costs due to longer distances, higher fuel prices, greater demand, limited port facilities and decreased carrier competition due to mergers.

Career Pathways in Logistics

Entry-level and frontline jobs in logistics usually require a high school education and perhaps, some additional certifications such as the OSHA 10-hour Safety Card, Forklift Operator Certification and the Certified Logistics Associates and Technician (CLA and CLT) credentials. The more education earned (industry certifications and 2-year, 4-year and advanced degrees), the higher the position and salary. Below are some sample jobs and salaries for logistics workers from entry-level through management:

Entry-level and frontline jobs
material movers, packers and packagers, freight handlers
Average wage: $9.57 - $13.00 per hour

Frontline jobs
order pickers, receiving and shipping attendants
Average wage: $10.51 - $18.00 per hour

Frontline supervisor jobs
team leader, frontline warehouse supervisor
Average wage: $21.72 - $26.65 per hour

First level management
transportation coordinator, outbound operations manager, freight rate specialist
Average salary: $35,700 - $50,900 per year

Mid-level management
inventory control manager, transportation manager, warehouse operations manager
Average salary: $69,200 - $78,100 per year

Upper-management
director of logistics, vice president of logistics
Average salary: $138,000 - $192,000 per year

Source: Salary information from BLS.gov 2013

Supply Chain Logistics

Chapter 1

Companies use a wide variety of logistics data to make their operations more efficient.

- Customer expectations for much higher levels of responsiveness.

For these reasons, distribution centers play a more vital role than ever. Under the influence of e-commerce, supply chain collaboration, quick response and Just-in-Time, logistics companies today must: [11]

- Handle and store more items
- Perform smaller transactions more often
- Provide more product and service customization
- Offer more value-added services
- Process more returns
- Receive and ship more international orders

At the same time, companies today have:

- Less time to process an order
- Less margin for error
- Less skilled, English-speaking personnel

Cost Effectiveness and Productivity Enhancement

To remain competitive, every company operating within the supply chain network must work continuously to reduce cost, while improving performance. For this reason, companies measure performance at each stage to determine the impact of operations on cost and performance.

Common Measures

These measurements include many factors, such as: productivity, quality, response time, operating costs, labor costs, inventory costs, shrinkage, expenses, damage, depreciation, capital costs, asset recovery and financing.

Chapter 1

Supply Chain Logistics

The added complexity of supply chain logistics is further increasing the importance of effective cost and performance measures. Materials management has a tremendous influence on the ultimate cost of a product because it handles the total flow of materials within an organization and between that organization and its customers.[12] The objective is to be able to deliver what customers want, when and where they want it, and to do so at minimum cost.

Many companies use performance measures for each of the major tasks within supply chain logistics. The performance of front-line workers can affect each of these measures. Here are some examples:

- *Customer response.* Order cycle time is the time it takes to process an order from the time the order is received from the customer until the order is delivered. This is a key factor in measuring customer service and maintaining customer loyalty. The quality of the product at time of delivery and the accuracy of the invoicing is also vital to good customer service.

- *Warehousing and Distribution.* There are many standards that warehouses and distribution centers use to track their productivity. These vary depending on the size, complexity of the product line and individual company policies. Some of the more common measurements are: units per hour, line items per hour, cases per hour, pallets per hour and labor cost per case.

- *Quality* must still take precedence over productivity. It doesn't do much good to get the product out the door in a hurry if it's wrong when it gets there.

Terms To Know

Cross-docking
The process of moving items directly from an incoming trailer or container to an outgoing trailer or container with little or no storage time in between.

Demand
A need for a particular product or component.

Distribution centers
A warehouse with finished goods and/or service items.

Order processing
The activity required to administratively process a customer's order and make it ready for shipment or production.

Packaging
Materials surrounding an item to protect it from damage during transportation. The type of packaging influences the danger of such damage.

Receiving
The function encompassing the physical receipt of material, the inspection of the shipment for conformance with the purchase order (quantity and damage), the identification and delivery to destination, and the preparation of receiving reports.

Supply Chain Logistics

Chapter 1

Terms To Know

Stock
1) Items in inventory.
2) Stored products or service parts ready for sale, as distinguished from stores, which are usually components or raw materials.

Supply
1) The quantity of goods available for sale.
2) The actual or planned replenishment of a product or component. The replenishment quantities are created in response to a demand for the product or component or in anticipation of such a demand.

Supply chain
The global network used to deliver products and services from raw materials to end customers through an engineered flow of information, physical distribution, and cash.

Warehouse
Facilities used to store inventory.

- *Transportation productivity* is usually measured separately: cartons delivered per mile driven, total cost per mile, cost per stop on the delivery route, cost per carton delivered, etc. Trailer utilization and on time delivery are also used as metrics for transportation.

Logistics Workforce Productivity Indicators

Productivity is a critical measure of performance throughout supply chain logistics. It directly affects a company's competitiveness, reputation and profitability. In turn, it affects workforce compensation levels.

While productivity is undeniably a critical part of any distribution operation, it should again be stressed that productivity must not sacrifice quality. Efficiency at order fulfillment is the main productivity measure for logistics. Thus, the output of the logistics workforce is typically measured in orders.[13]

Supply Chain Logistics

Foundational Knowledge:
For Frontline Workers

Chapter 1:
Global Supply Chain Logistic

Chapter 2:
The Logistics Environment

Chapter 3:
Material Handling Equipment

Chapter 4:
Safety Principles

Chapter 5:
Safe Material Handling & Equipment Operation

Chapter 6:
Quality Control Principles

Chapter 7:
Work Communication

Chapter 8:
Teamwork & Good Workplace Conduct to Solve Problems

Chapter 9:
Using Computers

OVERVIEW OF CHAPTER

The purpose of this chapter is to explain the logistics environment from the perspective of a frontline material handling worker. Frontline workers play a critical role in the supply chain because they are the people who physically move materials. This chapter will explain logistics facilities, security requirements and regulations, warehouse layouts and types of docks.

OBJECTIVES

When you have completed this chapter, you should be able to do these things.

1. **Identify** major security requirements applicable to the logistics environment

2. **List** four main initiatives which improve international logistics security

3. **Cite** examples of how logistics activities impact the environment

4. **Cite** two common warehouse layout options

5. **Describe** different types of docks

Supply Chain Logistics

Chapter 2

Security Requirements in Logistics

Protection and security of materials and information are important concerns of any facility within the supply chain. Whether it is securing a warehouse or ensuring a safe distribution route, security is always a priority. The requirements of securing a facility are similar whether it is a large warehouse, a shipping yard or a production site.

Securing Facilities

The very nature of the supply chain presents many security issues. Large vehicles require access to warehouses and distribution centers 24 hours a day. Employees, customers, suppliers, drivers, maintenance and repairmen all need access at different times during the day.[1] The following are some basic security measures that help increase security at these facilities.

The facilities within a supply chain network include:

- *Fences.* A high fence around the entire facility, yard or docking area creates a barrier to possible intruders.

- *Gates.* Many facilities use electric gates which can be activated remotely or by using special access cards. Others use manned gates where entering personnel are checked by security guards before gaining access to the area.

- *Security guards.* The most basic form of security posts guards at critical access points.

- *Lights.* Keeping an area well lit can be a major deterrent to would-be thieves.

- *Closed circuit television (CCTV).* Modern technology allows one security guard or office to monitor multiple access points from a central location.

Companies may use various methods to secure their logistics operations.

Supply Chain Logistics

Chapter 2

- *Alarm systems.* Depending on the value of the materials, alarm systems can include anything from a simple alarm to an integrated system which notifies police immediately and silently if unwanted access occurs.

Personnel Security

Another aspect of security depends on limiting access to certain areas or to an entire facility. This helps ensure that only trained workers who have a purpose in being there can get in. The simplest way to achieve this is with locks and keys. Modern technology has created alternatives to using an actual lock and key.

Identification badges. Employees need to have access to certain areas, but may not require access to the entire facility. Many facilities use entry locks activated by identification badges. The worker swipes an ID badge and gains entry into the facility or specific locations within the facility. Some systems track which ID badges have been used to access the site throughout the day.

Voice recognition. Another method of identifying personnel is voice recognition. A person speaks into a phone or receiver. A computer recognizes the information and takes appropriate action. Usually voice recognition is used for short transmissions such as password or yes and no questions. It can be used by approaching trucks to obtain daily access codes, or it can be used similarly to ID badges.

Did You Know?

$10 billion per year is stolen...

...from shipping and receiving docks in the U.S. So how do companies protect their employees, merchandise and property?

The greatest risk of cargo theft is during loading and unloading operations. For this reason, companies usually have tighter security in these areas of a warehouse.

Some common security measures for docks are:

- Restricting access to authorized personnel
- Requiring that employees and truck drivers have proper identification
- Having supervisors or security guards perform random checks
- Using container seals that are difficult to reseal once opened
- Using security systems that include badges, cameras, gates, etc.
- Not leaving loads or merchandise unattended during loading and unloading process or when visitors are present

Supply Chain Logistics

Chapter 2

C-TPAT Benefits Companies

C-TPAT has more than 10,000 partners that span the globe. Those partners represent over 50% (by value) of all goods imported into the United States. According to a University of Virginia study in 2007, partner companies reported the following benefits of membership:

- Decrease in supply chain disruptions
- Decrease in wait times for carriers at border
- Reduce time and cost in getting cargo released by CBP
- Reduce penalties
- Improve security for workforce
- Reduce cargo theft
- Access to FAST program
- Reduce insurance rates

Equipment Security

Just as it is necessary to monitor who has access to different areas of a facility, it is also important to restrict access to various types of equipment used in moving materials and loads around a facility or yard. To ensure that only authorized workers have access to various equipment and machinery, companies may install a screening system which requires the operator to swipe an ID card or enter an access code in order to use the equipment.

International Security: Rules and Regulations

Since the terrorist attacks on the United States of September 11, 2001, the global approach to supply chain security has changed significantly. It has brought about new international standards for logistics security, not only in this country but also around the world. In this section, major initiatives and rules that have been enacted to help protect against terrorist attacks and eliminate vulnerable links within the supply chain will be explored.

Customs-Trade Partnership Against Terrorism (C-TPAT)

C-TPAT was the first major global supply chain security initiative. It is a voluntary system established by the United States Bureau of Customs and Border Protection (CBP). Its chief goal is to create an environment of close co-operation between U.S. importers, carriers and international exporters to the United States.[2]

To participate in the Partnership, companies must conduct a comprehensive supply chain security assessment, submit a security profile to CBP and develop and implement a program to continually improve security. Companies are also required to communicate C-TPAT guidelines to other companies in their supply chain.

Supply Chain Logistics

Chapter 2

Today, over 10,000 companies are enrolled in the program. These include U.S. importers, U.S./Canada highway carriers; U.S./Mexico highway carriers; rail and sea carriers; licensed U.S. Customs brokers; U.S. marine port authority/terminal operators; U.S. freight consolidators; ocean transportation intermediaries and non-operating common carriers; Mexican and Canadian manufacturers; and Mexican long-haul carriers. These 10,000-plus companies account for over 50 percent (by value) of what is imported into the United States.

In addition to enhanced security for everyone in the supply chain, from supplier to customer, there are many benefits to member companies including:

- Reduced inspections, which means less border time and lower costs. Cargo from C-TPAT companies is less likely to be stopped and inspected for security and trade compliance. This can result in a savings of $500 per container, which is the average cost of border security reviews.

- Members of C-TPAT have access to a list of other members. This helps companies choose suppliers who are also enrolled in the program and enhances security within their link of the supply chain.

- There is a competitive advantage as well. Member companies are more likely to do business with other members than non-members.

- C-TPAT emphasizes self-policing. Once membership requirements have been met, CBP allows companies to monitor and work with each other.

- Members are also given access to FAST lanes (explained below) along the Mexican and Canadian borders.

Countries carefully control good that cross their borders

Free Trade Zones are areas within a country where barriers to trade such as tariffs and regulations are removed or relaxed to attract business and trade

Supply Chain Logistics

Chapter 2

Did You Know?

Key Facts about Containerized Shipping

- Each year, about 108 million cargo containers are transported through seaports around the world, constituting the most critical component of global trade.

- In fiscal year 2010, more than 10.1 million maritime shipments were reviewed in CSI Ports before arriving at United States seaports, an average of 27,600 a day.

- Almost 90 percent of the world's manufactured goods move by container, and about 40 percent arriving by ship.

- All trading nations depend on containerized shipping for the transportation of manufactured goods.

Free and Secure Trade (FAST)

The FAST program is a trade initiative between the United States, Canada and Mexico. It aims not only to guarantee safety and security but also to boost profits for each country. The main benefit is faster clearance to C-TPAT members' cargoes at these U.S. borders. Eligibility for the FAST program requires participants (carrier, drivers, importers and northern/southern border manufacturers) to submit an application, agreement and security profile depending on their role in the C-TPAT and FAST programs.[3]

Container Security Initiative (CSI)

The goal of the CSI is to focus first on the ports which send the highest volumes of container traffic into the United States and on the governments controlling those ports and to identify problems as early as possible. CSI operates in 58 ports worldwide, in regions including North, Central, and South America; the Caribbean, Europe, Africa, the Middle East; and throughout Asia. Currently, over 80 percent of all maritime cargo imported into the United States is subject to prescreening.

The four main elements of the CSI are:

- Establishing criteria to identify high-risk containers
- Pre-screening containers before they arrive at U.S. ports
- Pre-screening high-risk containers
- Developing more secure containers

Supply Chain Logistics

Chapter 2

Advanced Manifest Regulations

CBP requires both importers and exporters to send information electronically in advance of shipment. If the information is not submitted within the correct timeframe or is incomplete, the CBP can refuse the shipment or require additional inspections upon its arrival. The timings for advance manifests are different for different modes of transport. They are: 24 hours before loading for sea vessels, four hours before 'wheels up' from NAFTA and Central and South America above the equator for aircraft, two hours prior to arrival for rail, and one hour before arrival for trucks not covered by FAST. FAST truck carriers need to submit information only half an hour prior to arrival.[5]

Interconnection Security Agreement (ISA)

The Interconnection Security Agreement is federally mandated for any system, contractor or agency that touches the federal network, including those systems connected to CBP. ISAs are intended to minimize security risks and ensure the confidentiality, integrity, and availability of government information, as well as the information that is owned by the external organization that has a network interconnection with the government. Network interconnection is defined as the direct connection of two or more IT networks for the purpose of sharing data and other information resources.

Reduce:
The amount of waste generated, the amount of packaging used or the amount of energy used.

Reuse:
Items that can be used more than once such as pallets, certain types of packaging materials, etc.

Recycle:
Items that cannot be reduced or reused

Supply Chain Logistics

Chapter 2

Environmental Impact of Logistics Activities

There are different ways in which supply chain activities affect the environment, including waste management, pollution (noise, water and air), spillage and conservation. The International Organization of Standardization (ISO) 14000 series of standards outlines a system for companies to help ensure the best measures are being taken to protect the environment at each link of the supply chain. These standards provide businesses with an outline for managing environmental issues. The managers of the business are then responsible for setting guidelines and training workers to implement best work practices in accordance with those standards.

We will briefly discuss methods used and government regulations imposed upon industry to ensure minimal environmental impact. The government body responsible enforcing these regulations in the United States is the Environmental Protection Agency (EPA).

Government Regulation

The federal government, as well as many state governments, has enacted several regulations which affect the supply chain including:

- *The Clean Water Act* and the *Clean Air Act* regulate industrial waste disposal and other activities that result in contamination of the air and water. These laws regulate the types and amounts of waste or by products that can be released into the air or dumped into water supplies. Clean Water also regulates what can be dumped in areas where harmful chemicals may seep into ground water.

- *The Superfund* is the common name for a the Comprehensive Environmental Response, Compensation and Liability Act (CERCLA) which established a multi-billion dollar fund to pay for remediation of toxic waste sites left by companies that are unwilling or unable to pay. The same set of laws also creates liability for a broad spectrum of parties, such as prior owners or operators of sites that are currently contaminated, even if the pollution was legal when it occurred.

- *The National Environmental Policy Act* requires the federal government to consider environmental impact via an environmental impact assessment before taking any significant action, such as building a highway.

Each of these measures impacts the supply chain worker: through emission regulations for trailer trucks; hazmat disposal guidelines or additional training for employees who work with substances; and the handling of materials that could pose a threat to the environment if handled improperly.

Hazardous Materials

A Hazardous Material (hazmat) is a "substance or material that the U.S. Department of Transportation (USDOT) has determined is capable of posing an unreasonable risk to health, safety and property when transported in commerce". The term includes materials designated by USDOT in the official hazmat tables and regulations such as hazardous substances, hazardous wastes, marine pollutants, elevated-temperature materials etc.

Chapter 2

Supply Chain Logistics

A Hazmat Employee is any person who directly affects the safe transportation of such materials or substances. This not only includes the manufacturing of hazmats, but also includes any handling, loading, unloading or testing of hazmats, manufacturing of hazmat containers, preparing hazmats for transport or operating a vehicle used to transport hazmats.

The USDOT is the primary agency responsible for developing and enforcing hazmat rules and regulations. These regulations pertain mostly to transport of hazmats. They write regulations, receive comments from industry and the public, and then publish the regulations as a "Final Rule" with an effective date for compliance. This gives companies that will be affected by the new rule time to make the necessary adjustments to their equipment or operations.

Companies and individuals involved in the transport of hazmats must register and pay a fee to conduct business. The company then receives a certificate of registration from USDOT. After a motor carrier registers, it receives a permit and must certify that it has a security plan that complies with PHMSA standards.

The types of materials that require a company to register as a hazmat transporter include:

- Radioactive materials
- Explosives (more than 55 pounds)
- Toxic-by-inhalation materials
- Liquefied natural gas

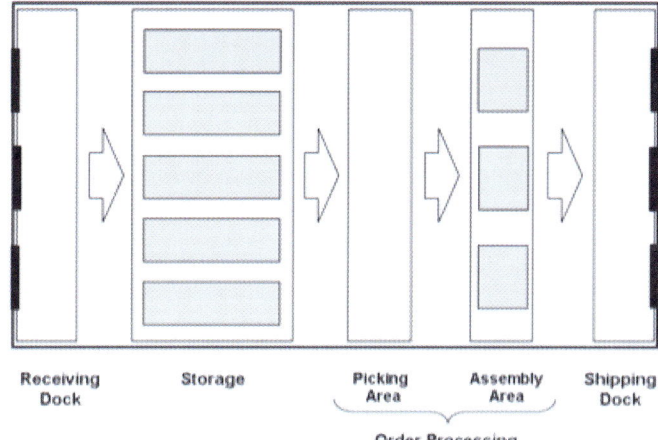

Linear warehouse layout

Supply Chain Logistics

Chapter 2

Recycling

Another way that companies in the supply chain can work to have less of an impact on the environment is recycling. There are three basic tiers of solid waste management put forth by the EPA: [7]

- *Source reduction* – reducing wastes at their source prevents them from getting into the waste stream.

- *Recycling* – through the recycling process, products that would otherwise become waste are collected, separated and used to make another product.

- *Incineration and land filling* – these are considered less desirable ways to handle waste. Indeed, one goal of reuse and recycling programs is merely to reduce the amount of material that is incinerated or dumped at landfills.

Physical Layout of Logistics Environment

Since most facilities that have similar functions within the supply chain also have similar designs, we now review the basic layouts of different types of facilities in the world of logistics.

Warehouses and Distribution Centers

Most warehouses and distribution centers are organized according to activity. In any of these facilities there will be a receiving dock, a storage area, a picking area, a staging area and a loading dock.

There are two common designs: linear which places the receiving dock at one end and follows a straight line to the loading dock at the other end of the building; and U shaped, which folds the linear model to allow a common dock to serve as both the receiving and shipping area.

The storage areas of warehouses and distribution centers may vary significantly based on the type of product and the type of equipment that is used. Most large operations will have some rack storage, some bulk storage and an area where they handle repack or small package goods.

Many distribution centers are nothing more than docks with a staging area. These centers are normally associated with truck terminals or "break build" points where the product is brought in for consolidation and immediately turn around for delivery. These are basically cross-dock functions and are commonly used for breaking down containers from inbound ports.

Facility Design

The key elements of facility design in terms of logistics are as follows:

- *Space.* The space available in a facility is more than just floor space. Warehouses and distribution centers are measured in cubic feet. That means that a building's capacity depends not only on the square footage available but also on how high the goods can be stored. Warehouses that carry many line items and types of products tend to use racks because it allows them to take full advantage of high ceilings and store a lot of different items without having to re-handle the product.

- *Accessibility.* Workers must be able to retrieve the materials with a minimum amount of effort. The best facilities are those that provide 100% accessibility for items retrieved most often. 100% accessibility means that no other goods have to be moved to reach a specific item. If several different items are

Supply Chain Logistics

Chapter 2

stored in the same area, each product should be accessible with minimal difficulty.[8]

This is one of the advantages of using racks for storage. It takes more time to put away and retrieve goods, but it does improve the ability to handle a lot of items. Rack storage also provides better protection for fragile items, rather than storing pallets on top of pallets that can damage items and offer less stability.

- *Throughput*. The volume of goods expected to move through a warehouse is also an important consideration. A high-volume distribution center that does not require significant bulk storage options will have different design requirements than a low-volume warehouse that serves primarily as a storage facility.

Flush docks are the most common type of dock in the U.S."

Docks

There are different types of docks, but all serve the same purpose – to provide a point of access for the receipt and delivery of goods into and out of warehouses, distribution centers and final points of destination.

Flush Docks

Today, flush docks are by far the most commonly used dock designs in the United States. This means that the outside wall of the building is flush with the face of the dock, or more basically, there is a hole in the building wall with a dock door and seal. The truck backs up to the wall and is secured against the seal. The trailer remains outside the building.

Open docks like this one are rarely seen in large logistics operations"

Open Docks

The least expensive dock is the open dock. It consists of a platform that extends out from the exterior building wall. All unloading and loading takes place on the platform outside the building. Safety is a

Supply Chain Logistics

Chapter 2

Terms To Know

Container Security Initiative (CSI)
A program of the U.S. government which seeks to ensure that containers entering the country's ports are scanned and deemed safe before departing their country of origin.

Customs-Trade Partnership Against Terrorism (C-TPAT)
A voluntary system established by the U.S. Bureau of Customs and Border Protection with the primary goal of creating and environment of close cooperation between U.S. importers, carriers and international exporters to the United States.

Free and Secure Trade (FAST)
An agreement between the United States, Canada and Mexico which aims to speed transport of goods between countries while ensuring safety and security of the general population.

Hazardous material (hazmat)
Any substance or material capable of posing and unreasonable treat to the health and/or safety of the general population.

Recycle
1) The reintroduction of partially processed product or carrier solvents from one operation or task into a previous operation.
2) A recirculation process.

concern in bad weather because the platform and workers are exposed to the elements. Some open docks have a canopy to help prevent rain and snow from making the dock platform slippery and dangerous.

Enclosed Docks

Enclosed docks provide the most security from theft and the most protection from weather. An enclosed dock is like a large garage. The entire truck and trailer loading area is completely inside the building or sheltered area. At the outside of the facility, large doors allow trucks to have access to the dock area. Once inside the enclosure the actual dock can be an open dock platform or a flush dock. Enclosed docks must have adequate ventilation and drainage to ensure the safety of drivers and loaders.

Rail sidings

Rail sidings are usually located away from the normal shipping and receiving areas and will have a separate unloading and staging area. They also can be enclosed or exterior type bays. Rail sidings are quite often enclosed because of the equipment that is used to unload them and they tend to sit at the siding longer while waiting to be unloaded.

While we will cover safety in another unit, it is worth emphasizing that dock areas, whether receiving, shipping or rail, are by far one of the most dangerous areas in a distribution center. More serious accidents occur there than anywhere else. Lift trucks driving off the dock, trucks moving away from the dock during unloading because they were not properly secured, trailers tipping during the unloading process are just some of the dangers

Supply Chain Logistics

Foundational Knowledge:
For Front-line Workers

Chapter 1:
Global Supply Chain Logistic

Chapter 2:
The Logistics Environment

Chapter 3:
Material Handling Equipment

Chapter 4:
Safety Principles

Chapter 5:
Safe Material Handling & Equipment Operation

Chapter 6:
Quality Control Principles

Chapter 7:
Work Communication

Chapter 8:
Teamwork & Good Workplace Conduct to Solve Problems

Chapter 9:
Using Computers

OVERVIEW OF CHAPTER

The purpose of this chapter is to explain various types of material handling equipment from the simplest hand truck to the most complex automated systems. Different modes of transportation, types of facilities and types of products require diverse types of equipment to move products throughout the supply chain. This chapter will introduce the most commonly used equipment and explain how it is used.

OBJECTIVES

When you have completed this chapter, you will be able to do these things.

1. **List** examples of manually operated equipment
2. **List** types of lift trucks
3. **List** types of loading dock equipment
4. **Describe** function and types of conveyors
5. **Identify** common automated systems used in material handling

Supply Chain Logistics

Chapter 3

A two-wheel dolly is used to move small volumes of boxed materials

Pallet jacks move only pallet at a time

Types of Equipment

There is a large variety of material handling equipment used today, ranging from simple hand trucks to sophisticated wire-guided turret trucks that cost as much as $60,000 each. This chapter covers equipment most commonly used in the supply chain process. However, each operation may have unique requirements for special handling.

Manually Operated Equipment

Hand trucks (two-wheel dolly). Hand trucks are generally used to move small items short distances in places like storage and parts rooms. They are not useful when large quantities of products need to be moved in a short amount of time or when products have been palletized.

Platform trucks (picking carts). Platform trucks are used in confined spaces for picking items that will be put on a conveyor and sent to the shipping area. Like a hand truck, platform trucks usually require the worker to manually place the products on the platform.

Pallet jacks. Pallet jacks are primarily used to move single pallets of products short distances or in areas where space is a constraint (i.e., moving single pallets inside a trailer or container). They can be manual or battery powered. The front wheels are imbedded in forks that are rolled under a pallet. A hydraulic jack raises the pallet just off the floor.

Chapter 3

Supply Chain Logistics

Industrial Fork Trucks / Lift Trucks

There are many different styles of lift trucks that are designed to do a variety of tasks within material handling operations. They are powered by electricity, propane or gasoline and have different characteristics depending on the types of loads they will carry.

Electric trucks are the most widely used for several reasons. They are easy to maintain, more environmentally friendly and much quieter than propane or gasoline trucks. Virtually all stand-up equipment in use today is electric powered. On the other hand, propane, gasoline and electric sit-down fork trucks are used throughout the supply chain.

Propane trucks are more common than gasoline trucks because they are more environmentally acceptable. Propane trucks can travel faster and handle heavier loads than electric trucks. Propane and gasoline trucks are normally used on docks or open areas where there is more room and ventilation. They can also be used outside very effectively and are not affected by weather like an electric truck can be.

Types of Lift Trucks

There are many types of lift trucks available which allow for different levels of maneuverability.

Electric Pallet Trucks. There are three primary types of electric pallet trucks, a single pallet truck where the operator walks along with the truck as it moves. This truck moves at about 3 mph. The other two types single pallet rider and double pallet rider trucks allow the operator to ride on the front of the truck as it moves. Rider trucks operate at about 7

Think About It!

Forklift accidents are a leading cause of injury in logistics.

According to OSHA, forklifts cause 85 deaths per year in the United States. There are almost 35,000 accidents that result in serious injury and over 60,000 that are classified as non-serious.

There are many types of powered industrial trucks. Each type presents different operating hazards. For example, a sit-down, counterbalanced high-lift rider truck is more likely than a motorized hand truck to be involved in a falling load accident because the sit-down rider truck can lift a load much higher than a hand truck. Workplace type and conditions are also factors in hazards commonly associated with powered industrial trucks. For example, retail establishments often face greater challenges than other worksites in maintaining pedestrian safety. Beyond that, many workers can also be injured when lift trucks are inadvertently driven off loading docks; lifts fall between docks and an unsecured trailer; they are struck by a lift truck; or they fall while on elevated pallets and tines.

Source: OSHA Website; https://www.osha.gov/SLTC/poweredindustrialtrucks/; August 2013

Supply Chain Logistics

Chapter 3

Counterbalance Forklift

Charging station for battery operated forklifts

Narrow aisle truck

mph. Double pallet rider trucks are often used for picking full cases in large warehouses with long picking aisles, and the picking is only done on floor level.

Narrow Aisle. Narrow aisle trucks are mainly used in rack areas because they do not require wide aisles as a counterbalance truck does (e.g., 8-ft aisles instead of 10-ft aisles). This means that more goods can be stored in a smaller area. Narrow aisle trucks are more expensive and usually have a standing operator platform. They have a small turning radius and load support via straddle and reaching capabilities.

Very Narrow Aisle trucks have been developed more recently to make better utilization of cubic space. This type of truck is either wire guided or rail guided and uses a turret truck that can rotate 180 degrees to place or retract loads or cases from both sides of the rack. Very often these rack modules stack five or six high pallet loads, 32- to 35-feet high. For this reason, these modules require very flat floors because the tolerances on equipment going that high are very tight. This set up is also very expensive to install, so it is rarely used.

Counterbalance. This term refers to the weight of the truck balancing the weight of the load keeping the truck from tipping over.

Stand-up counterbalanced lift truck. As suggested by the name, the driver on this truck stands while driving and operating the vehicle, which allows better visibility of the objects being moved.

Sit down counter balanced truck. This is probably the most common piece of equipment in warehouses. These trucks can be electric, propane or gasoline, are rated to handle up to 6,000 pounds, and are most

Supply Chain Logistics

Chapter 3

often used in high-volume shipping and receiving operations. They may also be referred to as fork lifts, fork trucks or lift trucks.

Order picker. This truck allows the operator to be lifted with the load to rack locations, which allows for picking from (usually) less than full pallet loads.[1]

Sideloader. A sideloader is usually used to handle greater-than-pallet-sized loads. The forks on the sideloader are mounted perpendicular to the direction of travel to allow for side loading and straddle load support.[2]

Carton Clamp Trucks. Carton clamp trucks are widely used in many warehouses for moving large bulky items typically stored on the floor in "bulk locations." These trucks are equipped with large rubber-lined paddles (4' x 6') that grip the carton using hydraulic pressure. This clamp attachment can be mounted on a standard forklift if it has the capacity to handle it.

Specialized equipment. Some equipment is specialized to handle specific types of products and packaging. Many lift trucks have a variety of attachments that can be easily switched out to accommodate different items, such as pallets or barrels. This allows companies to have one piece of equipment with multiple uses rather than having to have a dedicated piece of equipment for each different type of item. Examples include: slip sheet, carton clamp and roll clamp attachments which can be put on counterbalanced equipment.

Yard lift. A yard lift is a fork lift truck equipped with pneumatic tires that allow for operation on rough areas without jostling the load.

Order picker

Forklift that can be used outdoors

Supply Chain Logistics

Chapter 3

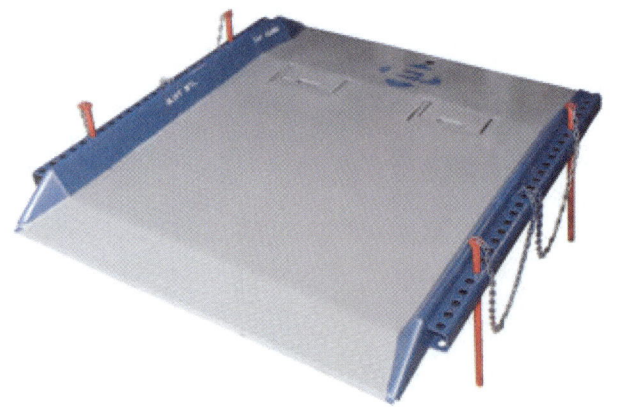

Dock board

A sorter conveyor with scanner.

Loading Dock Equipment

In order for industrial lift trucks and manual moving equipment to be used in loading and unloading, special equipment is required to allow the worker to push or drive the vehicle onto the dock, trailer or staging area.

Scissor lift or portable platform. This can be a portable or stationary device that lifts a platform to the height of the trailer or railcar deck. The worker drives onto the lift at ground level and then is lifted to the loading platform to pick up the load.

Dock board/plate. If the carrier vehicle deck is the same height as the warehouse doors, workers can bridge the gap with dock boards and drive or walk onto the vehicle for loading and unloading. Hydraulic dock plates can have capacities of up to 30,000 lbs. Yard ramps are similarly used in the yard to allow vehicles to drive from the yard onto a trailer or container.

Conveyors

Conveyors are typically used to move products over short distances, such as in loading and unloading.

Gravity conveyors. Gravity conveyors are the most basic and least expensive type of conveyor. They consist of metal bars with wheels or rollers attached. The conveyor is positioned at an angle allowing gravity to roll the container from one end to the other. They can be permanent or portable. The basic gravity conveyors are:

- Gravity wheel conveyors
- Roller conveyors
- Accordion wheel conveyors (these can be folded and rolled for easy storage when not in use)

Chapter 3

Supply Chain Logistics

Powered conveyor. These types of conveyors are powered using belts, chains and motors to drive the rollers. This allows packages to be moved horizontally on a flat plane or vertically.

Automated Conveyor Systems

Automated conveyor systems can be used to move materials throughout a facility with little or no human involvement.

Conveyor sorting systems are used to sort full cases or repack cartons down specific shipping lanes. The cases may come from several areas in the warehouse and are automatically sorted by use of a bar code. These are very efficient systems that can sort up to 4,000 cases per hour with incredible accuracy.

Vertical Reciprocating Conveyors (VRCs). To move materials vertically, warehouse designers use a VRC. The conveyor has buckets or fixed arms that grab the product and move it up or down to a different level.

Overhead Handling Equipment

To maximize space usage even more, some facilities use overhead handling equipment that moves items above the facility floor.

Overhead traveling conveyor. Carriers travel on motorized rails above the factory floor.

Overhead crane and hoist. These are sometimes used in battery changing operations or in maintenance departments but are generally not used in other warehouse or distribution center operations.

Another type of sorter with tilted trays

This is a vertical carousel with bins for small parts that rotate vertically to bring the correct items to the level of the order picker.

Supply Chain Logistics

Chapter 3

Gantry crane

An AGV with forks

Overhead traveling cranes. These devices are simple in design and follow a fixed path for travel. The overhead crane consists of four basic components.

- *Runways.* The track on which the crane travels.
- *End Trucks.* Runways are attached to the warehouse structure by means of carriers called end trucks.
- *Bridge beam.* The end trucks are placed at each end of a bridge beam.
- *Hoist.* A lifting mechanism placed on the bridge beam that is usually an electrically powered chain or wire rope hoist.[4]

Gantry. A gantry is a crane that also uses a bridge beam with a powered or manual hoisting mechanism. It often has wheels on the floor end for easy movement around the facility. The crane straddles a load to lift it. Since it is not on a track, this type of crane is not restricted to a fixed path.

Automated Systems

Automated Guided Vehicle (AGV). AGVs are guided by fixed paths such as rails, tracks or computer-aided guidance systems that utilize laser technology to guide the vehicle around obstacles. They do not require a person to operate them.

Automated storage/retrieval systems (AS/RS). This is a large, rail-running, robot-like vehicle called a storage/retrieval machine. The machine operates in an aisle between two storage rack structures, storing and retrieving loads.[5]

Shuttle Cars. Shuttle cars are sometimes used in place of AGVs to move materials across an AS/RS system. They can be in-loop type or reciprocating.

Terms To Know

Automated Guided Vehicle (AGV) System
A transportation network that automatically routes one or more material handling devices, such as carts or pallet trucks, and positions them at predetermined destinations without operator intervention.

Counterbalance
When the weight of a lift truck offsets the weight of the load it carries.

Dock board (dock plate)
A board or plate used to bridge the gap between a dock and trailer opening that allows people or equipment to move safely from one platform to another.

Supply Chain Logistics

Foundational Knowledge:
For Frontline Workers

Chapter 1:
Global Supply Chain Logistic

Chapter 2:
The Logistics Environment

Chapter 3:
Material Handling Equipment

Chapter 4:
Safety Principles

Chapter 5:
Safe Material Handling & Equipment Operation

Chapter 6:
Quality Control Principles

Chapter 7:
Work Communication

Chapter 8:
Teamwork & Good Workplace Conduct to Solve Problems

Chapter 9:
Using Computers

OVERVIEW OF CHAPTER

The purpose of this chapter is to provide an overview of the most common safety features and practices used in material handling operations. Employers and employees have responsibilities when it comes to safety. This chapter will explain safety practices and procedures used in modern logistics facilities.

OBJECTIVES

When you have completed this chapter, you will be able to do these things.

1. **Identify** the principle federal safety organizations and their fundamental requirements
2. **Identify** characteristics of a safe, clean and orderly work environment
3. **List** emergency safety procedures
4. **List** common safety markings and signs
5. **List** types of fire extinguishers

Supply Chain Logistics

Chapter 4

Safety is everyone's responsibility.

Federal Safety Organizations & Requirements

Government agencies play an important role in workplace safety. They develop standards, conduct research and help educate the public. Most of the safety practices described in this chapter are based on government standards.

OSHA

The Occupational Safety & Health Administration (OSHA) is the primary federal government agency devoted to workplace safety. OSHA was established in 1970 by the U.S. Department of Labor to "assure safe and healthful working conditions for working men and women." OSHA develops guidelines and issues regulations for safety and health standards and conducts inspections of workplaces for compliance with these standards.

OSHA sets and enforces thousands of safety standards. These cover everything from using ladders safely, to noise control, to storing hazardous materials. To ensure that these standards are met, OSHA officials inspect workplaces periodically. Employers can be fined or imprisoned for violating OSHA standards.

OSHA rules make a difference. Since OSHA was created, workplace deaths have been reduced by over half. Supply chain logistics material handling operations must comply with all health, safety and environmental policies and procedures defined by OSHA.

OSHA standards set only the minimum requirements. Supply chain logistics facilities may use additional guidelines from other government agencies or professional organizations.

Supply Chain Logistics

Chapter 4

USDOT

The U.S. Department of Transportation (USDOT) is the primary federal regulatory body for transportation safety. Although USDOT's safety responsibilities encompass all modes of transportation, the U.S. Coast Guard regulates safety of inland water carriers.

A current example of USDOT safety rules that directly affect logistics operations are the hours-of-service (HOS) safety rules. Effective January 2004, USDOT changed rules that had been in effect since 1939. The changes permit commercial motor vehicle drivers more time and opportunities for quality rest and restorative sleep to reduce the number of crashes caused by fatigued drivers.

FAA

The Federal Aviation Administration (FAA) has the primary responsibility for developing and enforcing air transportation rules and strives to improve the safety and efficiency of aviation. FAA issues various regulations related to air cargo handling around and within aircraft.

Other Federal Agencies

There are other federal agencies that have responsibilities related to the safe handling and movement of materials including:

- *The Federal Motor Carrier Safety Administration (FMCSA)* of USDOT is primarily focused on safety regulations for large trucks and buses. A recent FMCSA report on accidents involving large trucks indicated that driver behavior was much more likely than weather, road conditions or equipment factors to cause these accidents.

- *The Federal Railroad Administration (FRA)* has primary responsibility for safety in the U.S. railroad industry. FRA employs over 400 safety inspectors who investigate operating practices, tracks and structures, signal and train control issues, among others.

- *The Environmental Protection Agency (EPA)* is the federal agency that develops and enforces regulations protecting the land, air and water. EPA sets standards that directly affect the industrial workplace, including the disposal and handling of hazardous materials.

- *The National Institute for Occupational Safety & Health (NIOSH)* studies the causes of workplace injuries and illnesses and develops ways to help control hazards.

- *The Food and Drug Administration (FDA)* regulates labeling, packaging and safety of food products during production, transport and sale of the products.

State Agencies

Many states also set and enforce their own standards for workplace safety, commercial transportation and environmental preservation. According to OSHA, state workplace safety standards must be at least as effective as OSHA standards.

Supply Chain Logistics

Chapter 4

Companies are required to inform workers and visitors about possible workplace dangers.

Employees are required to follow safety rules set by their employers.

Safe, Clean & Orderly Work Environment

While federal agencies establish and enforce guidelines and regulations, safety is also a major responsibility of both employers and workers. Safety is a top priority in most workplaces today. Knowing the language, tools and practices of safety systems help make workers safer.

Responsible Employers

Employers are required and strongly motivated to create a safe and healthy workplace. Their responsibility to provide a safe working environment includes proper training, ample protection, safety equipment and hazard communication. Posting written warnings about unsafe conditions is one way to communicate hazards and encourage workplace safety.

General Requirements

To fulfill their safety responsibility, many employers have a safety committee that meets regularly and keeps a file of the notes of these meetings. The safety committee is an excellent source for corrective actions and accident reviews, as well as accident prevention plans. The safety committee only makes recommendations. It is the employer's responsibility to correct any unsafe or hazardous conditions

Supply Chain Logistics

Chapter 4

Employers must follow all local, state and federal laws regarding safety and the environment. They are required to keep a record and report to OSHA any workplace injury or illness that results in days away from work. They must also report any accident that results in medical treatment beyond basic first aid.

Employers are required by law to provide financial aid to workers who are injured on the job. This aid is called workers' compensation. It pays medical expenses and lost wages if the person cannot work. Job-related illnesses and death are also covered by workers' compensation.

Environmental accidents must be documented and reported to the appropriate government agency. These records must be made available to workers and worker representatives, including unions.

Training Requirements

Safety training is a major employer responsibility. Frequent refresher courses are essential to reinforce workplace safety practices. As new machines or processes are added, more training may be required. At a minimum, employers must teach workers about:

- Company first-aid and first-response procedures
- Emergency alarms and procedures
- How to inspect a work area and report possible safety risks
- Possible hazards in the workplace to help ensure personal safety as well as the safety of others
- Health and safety standards to ensure that quality problems are addressed correctly without impairing health and safety

Did You Know?

General Workplace Injury Statistics

- According to OSHA, four out of five compensable injuries from manual materials handling workers were lower back injuries. Three out of four of those injuries occurred while lifting.
- According to a 2002 Liberty Mutual Insurance report, accidents and incidents resulting from manual materials handling cost more than $10 billion.
- Direct compensation for overexertion injuries in the U.S. in 2006 was $12.4 billion, exceeding the compensation costs of injuries combined for the second and third categories, which include various types of falls.
- A 20-pound sack of flour held 20 inches in front of the body places about 400 pounds of compressive force on the lower spine.
- The back has 300 muscles, 33 vertebrae, and discs between the vertebrae. Discs are fibrous cartilage surrounding a soft, gelatinous material. Discs maintain alignment of the vertebrae and cushion the forces imposed by daily activities. Over a period of time, stresses can tear the fibrous outer casing of the discs. The discs have no blood supply for healing. The inner contents can leak out of a disc, causing it to narrow. The results can be pinching, deterioration of the joints, inflammation, and pain.

Source: Fast Facts, Office of Compliance, http://www.compliance.gov/wp-content/uploads/2010/08/Manual-Material-Handling-Fast-Fact-May-2010.pdf, August 2013

Supply Chain Logistics

Chapter 4

Workers are responsible for keeping their workstation clean.

Safety programs not only save lives but also save money. Accidents and illnesses cost employers and employees millions of dollars every year. This includes the cost of compensation payments, damaged products, clerical costs, lost work days and medical costs.

In addition to reducing accidents and injury, many safety practices also speed up processes and improve quality. For example, keeping floors clean and clear helps to prevent falls and to move material more quickly.[6]

Responsible Employees

"Safety is Number One" is an essential guideline for employees. Obviously, employees have a strong vested interest in preserving a safe work environment. By keeping their own work areas well-organized, clean and free of clutter, workers help protect themselves and their co-workers against serious accidents or injury.

Throughout safety training, workers should stay focused and ask questions as needed. Following training, workers must make their own effort to remain informed and stay up-to-date on safety-related information.

Regular Inspections

Safety Inspections

Routine safety inspections are one way to determine if safety measures are working. They also help determine what improvements may be needed. Inspections can focus on a single workstation or an entire department. They can take place at any time and as often as necessary. If day-to-day safety practices are good, preparations for inspections are minimal.

Chapter 4

Supply Chain Logistics

Safety inspectors must know and understand OSHA regulations and company safety measures. They verify that all safety processes are being performed correctly. This can be accomplished by reading a company's safety policies and procedures. Problem areas should receive extra attention. These might include any equipment or process that has resulted in a high number of accidents or near misses.

Checklists can be helpful tools for safety inspectors. However, if something is not included on a checklist, it does not mean it is not hazardous. Checklists are used only as guides. If other hazards are found, they must be noted and addressed. They should also be added to the checklist for future inspections.

This factory has clearly marked pedestrian walkways for added safety.

Upon completing an inspection, findings are documented. Flaws are recorded so they can be corrected. Improvements from the last inspection are also noted.

Hazard analysis

Hazard analysis is sometimes referred to as job safety analysis. It is a process used to reduce the risk of hazards to an acceptable level. In a hazard analysis, each step of a job is studied in detail. By identifying possible hazards, corrections can be made to help reduce injuries and time lost due to injuries.

Employers conduct a hazard analysis to assess and eliminate possible dangers.

Once a task is broken down, each step is analyzed for hazards. A hazard analysis may indicate that workers should wear protective clothing when handling a new chemical product. This would avoid the worker being splashed with a potentially toxic substance.

CLA: Foundational Knowledge: Chapter 4 - Safety Principles | Page 51

Supply Chain Logistics

Chapter 4

If an accident does occur, employees and employers must report any injuries.

Employers post warning signs to help prevent accidents.

A hazard analysis requires many of the same skills used by a good detective. Asking questions, watching work closely and keeping an open mind are important. Logistics workers often have the greatest insights into the hazards of different materials and containers.

Correcting Hazards

Uncovering hazards and finding solutions are two big steps toward improved workplace safety. However, if unsafe conditions and practices are not corrected quickly and effectively, safety efforts will have been wasted. The best solution is to eliminate the hazard. This may involve changing the way a material is moved or using more automated equipment for handling certain kinds of material.

If elimination is not possible, the risk of injury or accidents must be reduced in other ways, such as requiring protective equipment or adding machine guards, warning lights and better signs. Changing standard operating procedures (SOPs) may also be necessary. SOPs are the step-by-step instructions that explain how to carry out work processes. Once hazard corrections are made, it is critical to share them with all the workers affected by the change.

Environmental Inspections

Either as part of a safety inspection or as a separate activity, an environmental inspection may be required. This involves checking for anything that may cause air, ground or water pollution. For example, a worker may check hazardous material containers for leaks or dents, or the worker may check for proper waste disposal.

Supply Chain Logistics

Chapter 4

Looking for environmental hazards involves many of the same techniques used in identifying safety hazards. This includes checklists and good observation skills. In fact, there is often overlap between safety and environmental issues. For example, a leak in a hazardous chemical container could cause air pollution. It could also threaten the health of workers who inhale or come in contact with it.

Complete and accurate record keeping is critical when conducting environmental and safety inspections. In fact, detailed documentation is often required by law. Inspection forms must be completed and filed according to company policies. If a hazard is identified, inspectors must follow correct policies for alerting supervisors and correcting the hazards.

Effective Reporting

Workers are the eyes and ears for safety and environmental protection in supply chain logistics. It is important to promptly report all safety issues to safety representative or employer.

Reporting Incidents

A safety or environmental incident includes anything that poses a potential hazard. Incidents can range from damaged automatic storage and retrieval equipment to a burned-out light bulb in a safety sign. Incidents also include near misses. These are incidents in which an accident almost occurred but did not. Near misses often serve as an important warning sign that something is wrong and needs to be changed. The sooner an incident is reported, the faster it can be addressed. Some companies require a written report to be filled. Others require that a safety representative or supervisor be notified.

Accident Investigating and Reporting

Accidents do happen. When they do, workers who are involved or who witnessed the accident have to participate in the reporting and investigation process. When an accident happens in the warehouse, an investigation will occur. This investigation may be conducted by a company safety officer, an OSHA inspector or a third-party investigator, depending upon the severity of the accident or injury:

A typical investigation process:

1. Establish the facts of the accident (time, individuals involved, witnesses, contributing factors, etc.)
2. Draw a sketch or diagram of the scene: this does not have to be an artist's sketch, but a simple drawing that shows the location of any people, equipment and hazards that were involved in the accident
3. Take photos of the scene
4. Interview witnesses and evaluate their statements compared to the scene and each other's statements
5. Determine the direct and indirect causes of the accident
6. Examine the standard operating procedures: SOPs are examined to determine if they were properly followed and to determine if it might be necessary to change procedures to prevent a similar accident in the future
7. Consult with experts or supervisors as necessary
8. Write up a report that clearly identifies the facts of the accident, causes and recommendations to prevent similar accidents in the future

Supply Chain Logistics

Chapter 4

With all of the equipment, dust and materials that are in a warehouse, it is important that the facility be properly ventilated.

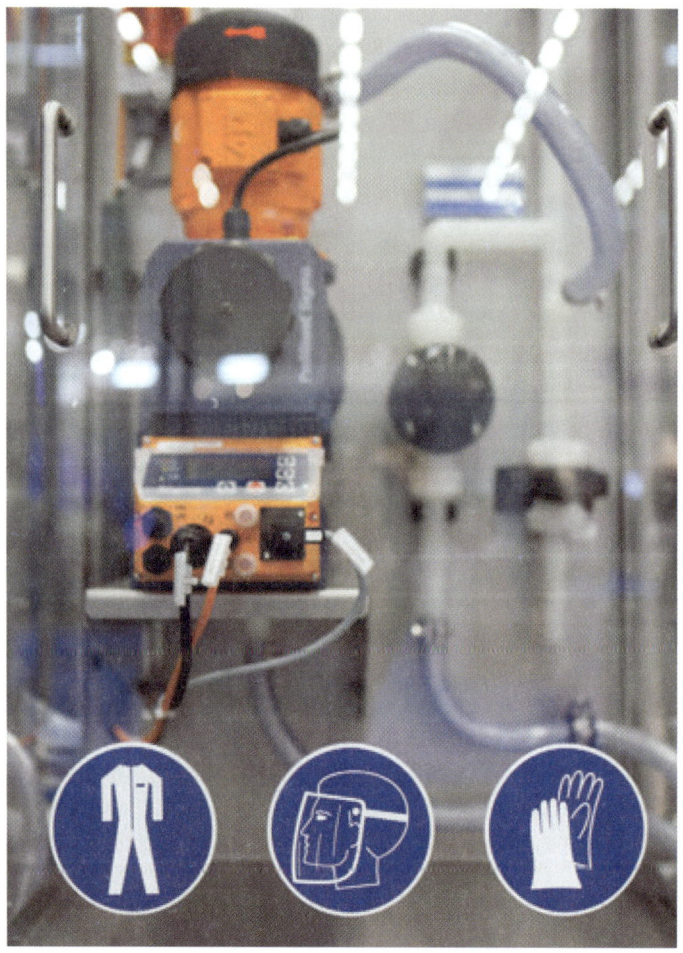

Some parts of the facility may require extra protection.

Reporting Accidents

Companies are required by law to keep records of serious accidents. They rely on workers to provide them with complete and accurate reports. These reports help investigators understand what caused a problem and how to prevent it from happening again.

If you are injured on the job, witness an accident or develop a job-related illness, notify a supervisor immediately. Once you have completed any required reports, request or make copies for your own files. Then, if your supervisor has not already done so, alert your safety representative or safety committee. They, too, can take action to correct the problem and prevent further injuries or incidents.

Well-designed Workplace Environment

Sound Construction

The integrity and strength of a facility's floors, walls, ceilings and roofs are essential elements of safety in the workplace.

Ventilation

Ventilation provides a way of circulating and refreshing the air. It is critical when working around hazardous materials and dust, and in confined spaces, crowded rooms or areas without windows. Exhaust fans, open windows and air conditioning systems are examples of ventilation systems. Employers are responsible for providing proper ventilation. If you suspect poor ventilation, notify your supervisor.

Supply Chain Logistics

Chapter 4

Ergonomics
The science of designing and arranging tools people use is called ergonomics. In the workplace, ergonomics is used to determine the safest and most efficient way to work in a particular space. It includes studying the lighting, tools, workstations and movements used when working. It also studies their effects on injury and illness.

Ergonomics has helped identify the types of activities that can cause injury or fatigue. These include repetitive motions, forceful exertions, vibrations and awkward working positions. These types of activities cause about one-third of all workplace injuries and illnesses. If any activity or repetitive motion causes continual discomfort, they may be able to correct the problem simply and prevent from becoming seriously injured or disabled.

Lighting
Poor lighting can hinder production quality and worker health. Dim work areas reduce the clear vision needed to produce products and conduct quality control. In turn, reduced vision contributes to accidents, eyestrain and vision problems. Employers are responsible for offering well-lit work areas, aisles, stairways, ramps and storage areas. Burned-out light bulbs should be reported and replaced promptly.

Exit Doors & Aisles
Exit areas must be clearly marked and not blocked. Time is critical during emergencies, and the time it takes to unblock an exit could cost a life. Aisles should be wide enough to allow workers to safely walk through the area. They also must remain as clear as possible. Forklift drivers should safely and promptly pull over their vehicles to permit passage through the aisles.

Large facilities often have specific walk ways for pedestrians throughout the building. These are identified with markings painted on the floor, and forklift drivers know to be cautious when operating in and around these areas.

Safety Markings
Companies use many types of safety signs and markings to communicate safety information in the workplace. These signs are usually color-coded to identify specific dangers.

Special Handling Storage Measures
It may be necessary to isolate certain types of stored products in separate areas. These may include hazardous chemicals, flammable materials or high-value items. This will allow management to better apply any special regulations regarding the safe handling of these materials.

Clean floors
Slips and falls are one of the top three causes of injuries in the workplace. Any spills or leaks should be cleaned immediately. In areas where water or chemicals are used for cleaning purposes (i.e. battery cleaning areas) drains must be provided to handle the runoff and contain any unwanted residue from the battery. Slip-resistant floors are often used in such areas.

Housekeeping
Housekeeping at work is about more than making the warehouse or dock look nice. Keeping work areas clean and uncluttered helps prevent serious accidents, including falls and fires. Housekeeping is an ongoing activity throughout the workday. Pallets should be neatly stacked no more than 8-ft high, waste packaging and rubbish should be placed

in an appropriate area, spillages of any kind should be cleaned promptly and fire exits should be free of any impediments.

Clear aisles

Aisles, walkways, stairways, storage areas and work surfaces that are clear of extraneous materials, debris and clutter are safer for everyone. Covered, fire-resistant containers reduce the dangers of fire. Quick cleanup of dust, loose wrappings, fibers and other small particles that can catch fire or explode also lowers accident risk. Clear walkways are also critical in the event of a fire or other emergency—workers must be able to exit the building quickly and easily.

Ladders and Scaffolds

Using a ladder or a scaffold to reach an item can be dangerous. Even a short fall can result in a serious injury. Some guidelines to prevent accidents include:

- Wear shoes with a minimum one-half-inch heel to ensure that feet catch on ladder rungs and prevent slipping.
- Before each use, inspect ladders and scaffolds for tight fasteners as well as broken rungs and side rails.
- Use short ladders and a fall-protection system on scaffolds.
- Use the right ladder or scaffold for the job. Fiberglass is often the safest material for ladders.

Color	Meaning	Used to Identify
Red	Danger, stop or emergency	Fire equipment, exit signs, panic buttons on machinery, containers for flammable materials, and signs for hazardous areas
Orange	Warning	Hazardous equipment or parts of a machine (e.g., parts of a machine that can cut or crush or electrical boxes with start and stop buttons)
Yellow	Caution	Tripping or falling hazard (used with black diagonal stripes
Blue	Information or caution	Safety signs, bulletin boards, out-of-order signs
White	Storage	Traffic flow (used alone or with black)
Green	Safety	First-aid stations, first-aid kits and safety equipment (used with white)
Magenta or Black on Yellow	Radiation caution	Indicates areas where radiation is present

Supply Chain Logistics

Chapter 4

- Use a full-body harness and an attached cord when riding in a mechanical lift basket.

Loading Docks

Loading docks are areas where materials and products are loaded and unloaded. They are often centers of much activity. There may be large vehicles, heavy loads being shifted and people working in a fairly small space. Loading docks can also be noisy, making it difficult to hear which can compromise safety.

The following devices and practices are designed to prevent loading dock accidents:

- Flashing lights and other warnings, such as audio signals, may indicate a vehicle is approaching or backing up.

- A wheel chock is a block placed in front of the back wheels of a truck or trailer to prevent the vehicle from moving away from the dock during loading and unloading.

- Most facilities are equipped with "dok-lok" devices that secure the trailer to the building and use a system of lights to indicate that the trailer is safe to enter or not.

Wheel chocks are used to help ensure that a trailer doesn't move during unloading.

- A secure ramp connecting a trailer or truck to the dock and preventing forklifts or workers from falling between the vehicle and the dock. These ramps are sometimes called bridge plates.

- Spacious and clean dock areas allow access to and movement by vehicles and people.

- Visibility and safe practices in dock areas are essential in avoiding falls over step edges.

- Some companies use marine and railroad loading docks. Ships and trains pull up to these docks to load and unload goods. These docks require special safety measures.

Supply Chain Logistics

Chapter 4

Class of Fire		Type of Flammable Material	Type of Fire Extinguisher to Use
Class A	▲	Wood, paper, cloth, plastic	Class A / Class A:B
Class B	■	Grease, oil, chemicals	Class A:B / Class A:B:C
Class C	●	Electrical cords, switches, wiring	Class A:C / Class B:C
Class D	★	Combustible switches, wiring, metals, iron	Class D
Class K	K	Fires in cooking involving combustible vegetable or animal oils and fats	Class K

Preventive and Emergency Safety Procedures

A fire can quickly become a tragedy. The best way to stop a fire is to prevent one from starting. However, in the event of an emergency, workers must be prepared. Work with all team members to conduct effective fire, safety and emergency drills.

Fire Prevention

Most material handling workers are exposed to flammable and combustible materials. These include boxes, pallets, protective coverings, dust and hazardous materials.

The following techniques help prevent fires.

- Cigarette, lighter and match use is banned near flammable or combustible materials.

- Flammable liquids are stored in approved, labeled and closed containers so liquid or vapor cannot escape.

- Flammable materials are not stored near any material that can make a fire worse. These materials include oxidizers such as peroxides.

- Spills involving flammable or combustible liquids or unidentified liquids must be reported immediately.

- Proper ventilation is essential to prevent the buildup of vapors that can catch fire.

- Tested and approved grounding techniques are used when transferring and transporting flammable or combustible liquids.

Supply Chain Logistics

Chapter 4

- Heat-producing equipment, such as burners, heat exchangers, boilers and stoves, are kept free of flammable residues. Flammables are not stored close to these pieces of equipment.
- Scraps and rubbish are disposed of regularly.

Fire Extinguishers

A fire extinguisher is a container filled with a fire-retardant material. There are different extinguishers for different types of fires. Using the wrong type of extinguisher can make some fires worse. Figure 4.4 shows the different types of extinguishers and the types of fires they are used to fight.

Safety within supply chain logistics facilities depends upon workers knowing fire-extinguisher locations, types, and uses. When using a fire extinguisher, operators should ensure that there is an escape route behind them. This will ensure a safe exit if the fire grows out of control. Use an extinguisher only if you have received proper training for its use.

When fighting small fires, workers are encouraged to follow the PASS sequence:

*P*ull the pin to unlock the fire extinguisher lever.
*A*im low, toward the base of the fire.
*S*queeze the lever to discharge the extinguishing agent.
*S*weep the hose back and forth across the fire.

Once used, fire extinguishers must be recharged. Regular inspection and maintenance of extinguishers is also critical. An extinguisher that is broken or empty is useless in an emergency. In some workplaces, workers are told not to try to put out a fire. Instead, they are to evacuate the premises, call 911 and leave the firefighting to trained personnel.

Supply Chain Logistics

Chapter 4

Terms To Know

Accident
An event causing injury, ill-health or property damage.

Ergonomics
Approach to job design that focuses on the interactions between human operator and such traditional environmental elements as atmospheric contaminants, heat light, sound, and all tools and equipment.

Grounding (electrical)
Connecting electrical equipment and wiring systems to the earth with a wire or other conductor to reduce the risk of serious electrical shock

Job hazard analysis
A technique that focuses on job tasks as a way to identify hazards before they occur. It focuses on the relationship between the worker, the task, the tools, and the work environment.

Near miss
A safety incident in which an accident does not occur, but came close to occurring.

Safety incident
An unplanned, undesired event that hinders completion of a task and may cause injury or other damage.

SOP
Standard operating procedure.

Fire Exits
During an emergency, efficient evacuation depends upon workers moving promptly and calmly towards the closest exits. They must know where all emergency exits are located. Many large companies conduct regular fire and safety drills to ensure that all workers know how to react in the event of an emergency.

Electrical Safety

Electrical equipment and power lines are dangerous if not handled properly. They can cause severe shocks, burns or even death. The body experiences electrical shock when it is part of the path through which electrical current flows. For example, touching a live wire and another wire of a different voltage can cause an electrical shock. Electrical shocks can cause severe injuries and death.

Many people believe that it is the amount of voltage that determines the danger of an electrical shock. However, the real danger is the rate and amount of current moving through the human body and the path the current takes through the body. This means that it is possible for a shock of 100 volts can be more deadly than one of 10,000 volts. The amount of current moving through the body depends on resistance factors. These include the wetness of the skin, the length of contact and whether the person is well grounded.

Electricity demands respect and caution.
To prevent shock, workers should:

- Alert supervisors or maintenance personnel of possible problems.

- Never open electrical enclosures unless authorized.

- Ground all electrical equipment.

- Do not use equipment if the electrical cord is frayed, cracked or damaged in any other way.[7]

Chapter 4

Supply Chain Logistics

OSHA makes sure that workers know their health and safety rights.

Supply Chain Logistics

Notes

Supply Chain Logistics

Foundational Knowledge:
For Frontline Workers

Chapter 1:
Global Supply Chain Logistic

Chapter 2:
The Logistics Environment

Chapter 3:
Material Handling Equipment

Chapter 4:
Safety Principles

Chapter 5:
Safe Material Handling & Equipment Operation

Chapter 6:
Quality Control Principles

Chapter 7:
Work Communication

Chapter 8:
Teamwork & Good Workplace Conduct to Solve Problems

Chapter 9:
Using Computers

OVERVIEW OF CHAPTER

The purpose of this chapter is to explain logistics safety. In addition to the basic concepts of safety learned in Chapter Four, frontline material handling workers need to know safety principles specifically related to material handling and equipment operation. This chapter will introduce the most common safety measures used in logistics facilities when handling materials.

OBJECTIVES

When you have completed this chapter, you will be able to do these things.

1. **List** basic safe material handling practices
2. **Identify** types, functionality and use of personal protective equipment
3. **List** equipment safety features
4. **Describe** the two basic types of maintenance

Supply Chain Logistics

Chapter 5

Basic Safe Material Handling Practices

Logistics workers must be knowledgeable and cautious about handling materials in all facilities within the logistics supply chain. Most of the materials are heavy, and some may be hazardous.

Various types of equipment are used in material handling. The simplest systems being manually operated equipment. Large operations generally require power equipment, the most common being the forklift truck. The modern forklift is a versatile piece of equipment with a number of fork replacement attachments enabling it to perform a wide variety of functions.

Vendors that make material handling equipment are responsible for providing detailed safety information. Workers must be well trained on the use of any piece of equipment that they may operate, including the safety processes involved in using the equipment.

Despite the increased use of automation and mechanical handling equipment in distribution centers and warehouses, there are still many potential hazards involved. The increased speed of operation required in modern logistics facilities has also created a new set of hazards.

Some of the hazards that are still very common include manual handling injuries, vehicle reversing incidents, unstable racking and personnel slipping, tripping and falling. This chapter focuses on safety processes related to manual material handling.

Supply Chain Logistics

Chapter 5

Definition

According to the U.S. Department of Labor, manual material handling is defined as: "Seizing, holding, grasping, turning or otherwise working with the hand or hands. Fingers are involved only to the extent that they are an extension of the hand, such as to turn a switch or to shift automobile gears."[1] In this text, manual material handling means that the worker's hands move individual containers or products manually by lifting, lowering, filling, emptying or carrying them.

Safety Issues Related to Manual Material Handling

Manual handling of containers may expose workers to physical conditions (e.g., force, awkward postures and repetitive motions) that can lead to injuries, wasted energy and wasted time. To avoid these problems, companies can directly benefit from improving the fit between the demands of work tasks and the capabilities of its workers. The variation in workers' abilities to perform work due to differences in age, physical condition, strength, gender and stature affect that fit.

Ensuring a good fit between tasks and capabilities can greatly benefit the workplace by:

- Reducing or preventing injuries
- Reducing workers' efforts by decreasing forces in lifting, handling, pushing and pulling materials
- Reducing risk factors for muscle and bone disorders (e.g., awkward postures from reaching into containers)
- Increasing productivity, product and service quality and worker morale
- Lowering costs by reducing or eliminating material handling bottlenecks, error rates or rejects, medical treatment, workers' compensation claims, excessive worker turnover, absenteeism and retraining

What to Look for

Manual material tasks may expose workers to physical risk factors. If these tasks are performed repeatedly or over long periods of time, they can lead to fatigue and injury. The main risk factors, or conditions, associated with the development of injuries in manual material handling tasks include:

- Awkward positions (e.g., bending, twisting)
- Repetitive motions (e.g., frequent reaching, lifting, carrying)
- Forceful exertions (e.g., carrying or lifting heavy loads)
- Pressure points (e.g., grasping or contact from loads, leaning against parts of surfaces that are hard or have sharp edges)
- Static postures (e.g., maintaining fixed positions for a long period of time)

Repeated or continual exposure to one or more of these factors initially may lead to fatigue and discomfort. Over time, injury to the back, shoulders, hands, wrists or other parts of the body may occur. Injuries of this type are known as musculoskeletal disorders, or MSDs.

In addition, poor environmental conditions, such as extreme heat, cold, noise and poor lighting may increase workers' chances of developing other types of problems.

Supply Chain Logistics

Chapter 5

Training

Workers need training and hands-on practice with new tools, equipment or work practices to make sure they have the skills necessary to work safely. Training is most effective when it is interactive and fully involves workers. Below are some suggestions for training for safer manual material handling training:[2]

- Provide hands-on practice when new tools, equipment or procedures are introduced
- Use several types of visual aids (e.g., pictures, charts, videos) of actual tasks in the workplace
- Hold small-group discussions and problem-solving sessions
- Give workers ample opportunity for questions

Employee Guidelines for Safer Lifting and Carrying

- Stretching is an appropriate part of a comprehensive ergonomic program. However, stretching must not be used in place of engineering and/or administrative improvements.
- Check for tags on loads.
- Always test the load for stability and weight.
- For loads that are unstable and/or heavy, follow management guidelines for:
  - Equipment use
  - Reducing the weight of the load
  - Repacking containers to increase stability.
- Plan the lift:
  - Wear appropriate shoes to avoid slips, trips and falls.
  - If wearing gloves, choose a size that fits properly. Depending on the material and the

Supply Chain Logistics

Chapter 5

number of pairs worn at once, more force may be needed to grasp and hold objects. For example, wearing a single pair of heat-resistant gloves can reduce your grip strength up to 40 percent. Wearing two or more pairs of gloves at once can reduce your grip strength up to 60 percent.
  - Lift only as much as can be safely handled alone.
  - Keep the lifts in the power zone (i.e., above the knees, below the shoulders, and close to the body), if possible.
  - Use extra caution when lifting loads that may be unstable.

- When lifting:
  - Get a secure grip.
  - Use both hands whenever possible.
  - Avoid jerking by using smooth, even motions.
  - Keep the load as close to the body as possible.
  - To the extent feasible use legs to push up and lift the load, not the upper body or back.
  - Do not twist the body. Step to one side or the other to turn.
  - Alternate heavy lifting or forceful exertion tasks with less physically demanding tasks.
  - Take rest breaks.

- Avoid lifting from the floor whenever possible. If a load must be lifted from the floor, do not bend at the waist.

- Use team lifting; mechanical assistance; a turntable; or other lifting and carrying assistance if available.

- Work within the power zone. Raise or lower the work surface.

- Store heavier or bulkier containers so that they can be handled within the power zone.

- Use angled shelving to improve access to containers.

Supply Chain Logistics

Chapter 5

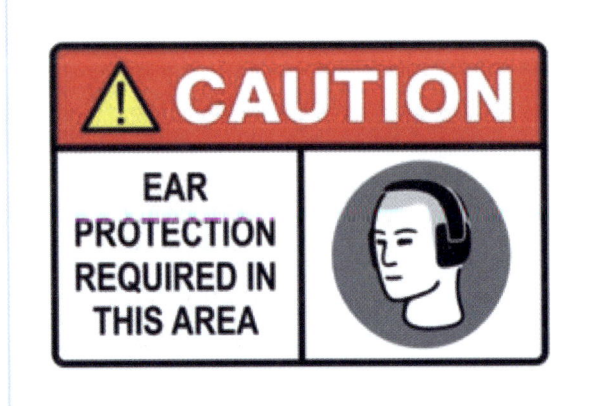

- Hold the container close to the body.
- Add extra handles for better grip and control.[3]

Personal Protective Equipment

Occupational Safety and Health Administration (OSHA) Requirements

OSHA's Personal Protective Equipment (PPE) standard ensures the use of gloves, safety goggles and hard hats—items that directly affect warehouses and distribution centers. Employers are required by the standard to perform a hazard assessment at the workplace to determine if employees should wear PPE. If so, the employer must put that requirement in writing, select the proper PPE and see that employees use it.

Any employee working in an area that the employer has determined to need PPE must receive training on what PPE is required, when it should be used, how to wear and adjust the PPE and how to maintain and dispose of the PPE. The employer must then certify that the employee has received and understands the training.[4]

Types of PPE

Head Protection

Falling objects, water, dirt and sparks can be a danger in supply chain logistics facilities. Protective helmets, usually called hard hats, protect against these hazards. Insulated hard hats offer additional protection. They are designed for workers exposed to electrical shock hazards.

Chapter 5

Supply Chain Logistics

Hand & Arm Protection

Burns, cuts, pinches and chemical or biohazard exposure are hazards that prompt hand and arm protection. Different types of gloves protect hands from specific hazards. Some protect against chemicals or electrical shock. Cut-resistant gloves protect against sharp tools or materials such as metal, glass or abrasive materials.

Lung Protection

Some airborne dust, fiber and particles put workers at risk for lung injury and illness. A dust mask, which is worn over the lower part of the face, filters out large particles. A respirator includes a face piece, hood or helmet with a replaceable cartridge. It filters smaller particles and dangerous fumes from the air.[5]

Foot Protection

The most common PPE is steel-toed boots. These are rugged shoes usually made of leather or a strong synthetic fiber. They have a steel plate in the front part of the boot that covers the front part of the foot. Even when every precaution has been taken, accidents do happen, and quality work boots can protect feet from falling or dropped items.

Eye/Face Protection

Safety goggles are used to shield the eyes from heat and impact hazards, chemicals and dust. Goggles should form a protective seal around the eyes, preventing objects or liquids from entering under or around the goggles. When fitted and worn correctly, goggles protect your eyes from hazardous

CLA: Foundational Knowledge: Chapter 5 - Safe Material Handling & Equipment Operation

Supply Chain Logistics

Chapter 5

These workers are performing an equipment safety check.

This worker is performing maintenance on a heavy loader.

substances. A face shield may be required in areas where workers are exposed to severe chemical hazards. Safety goggles may incorporate prescription lenses mounted behind protective lenses for individuals requiring vision correction. Take time to consider specific lens, frame, and ventilation options when selecting safety goggles.

Ear Protection

OSHA regulations require ear protection and annual training to be provided to employees who are exposed to noise at or above 85 decibels for an average 8-hour day. Ear protection can be in the form of earplugs that fit in the outer ear canal and form an airtight seal or earmuffs that fit over the entire outer ear to form an airtight seal (they will not seal around eyeglasses or long hair). Properly fitted earplugs and earmuffs reduce noise levels 15 to 30 decibels. In extremely noisy conditions, it may be necessary to wear earplugs and earmuffs together.

Safety Checks

Safe use of material handling equipment and loading equipment is important in any logistics system. Misuse of this equipment can be costly or even deadly. For example, one expert noted "in the United States, over 1,000 warehouse employees died from forklift-related incidents between 1980 and 2004."[6] One way of ensuring that equipment is safe is to monitor equipment regularly for any malfunction or hazard.

Material handling equipment must be regularly maintained and checked to ensure that workers are not injured when operating or working near the equipment. Depending on the frequency of use and potential dangers, safety checks may need to be performed daily or before each operation. Many of the vehicles and machinery used by logistics workers require training before operation of the equipment. The company or the manufacturer of the equipment usually provides this training. The manufacturer is responsible for providing safe operation information, and employers are responsible for ensuring that workers have sufficient understanding of how to operate the equipment safely. It is important that front-line workers do not operate equipment unless they have been trained to do so.

Equipment Safety Features

Logistics equipment may have safety features or you may need to employ safety devices before operating the equipment.

Restraints
Once trucks are positioned at the dock they must be restrained from further movement by means of wheel chocks or trailer restraints.

Communication lights
Similar to traffic signals seen on the street, communication lights can be either a two or three light device. They operate in pairs with one set of lights stationed on the interior warehouse wall at the dock doors and another set of lights on the exterior wall near each loading dock door.[7]

Interior communication lights
These lights serve to notify warehouse personnel of the location of trucks and railcars relative to the doors of the warehouse. Operated by personnel or by photo eyes, they register a vehicle's presence at the loading dock door or if the vehicle has been pulled away. A red light typically signals to the operator of a lifting device that there is no vehicle at the floor. A green light signals that there is a vehicle waiting and that it is safe to open the door.[8]

Exterior communication lights
A green light on the exterior door signals that it is safe to dock the vehicle. A red light signals the person positioning the vehicle that there is a reason not to pull up to or station a vehicle at that door.[9]

Capacity rating
Each type of equipment has a capacity limit based on weight and/or volume. Racks, for example, are given a capacity rating based on the strength of the components of the rack system. Placing too heavy or too large a load on a section of pallet rack is a safety risk to personnel because the rack may fail and fall. Damage may also occur to the product housed on the pallet rack.

Audible alarms
In addition to communication lights, some doors are equipped with alarms that sound when the door is about to open or close to warn workers to stand clear. Many powered material handling and transport vehicles are also equipped with back-up beepers.

Maintenance

In order to ensure safety and cost effective operations, routine maintenance must be performed on all types of logistics equipment. There are two basic types of maintenance, corrective and preventive.

Supply Chain Logistics

Chapter 5

Terms To Know

Corrective maintenance
The maintenance required to restore an item to a satisfactory condition.

Material handling
The movement of items from one point to another inside a facility or between facilities.

Personal Protective Equipment (PPE)
Equipment worn by workers to protect them from harm, including steel toed boots, gloves, goggles, ear plugs, etc.

Preventive maintenance
The activities, including adjustments, replacements, and basic cleanliness, that forestall machine breakdowns. The purpose is to ensure that production quality is maintained and that delivery schedules are met. In addition, a machine that is well cared for will last longer and cause fewer problems.

Corrective Maintenance
This is also known as equipment repair. It is dealing with a malfunction or failure after it has occurred.

Preventive Maintenance
Preventive maintenance is the care and servicing of equipment to ensure satisfactory operation and to provide for early detection of possible failures, defects or hazards. It usually involves scheduled maintenance checks to prevent a breakdown or malfunction before it occurs.

Operating Equipment Checklists
One form of preventive maintenance is an operating checklist. Logistics equipment must be maintained on a daily basis. An effective method of ensuring that all equipment is operating properly is to have an operator examine the machinery prior to use each day according to a predetermined checklist of critical items. The manufacturer of the equipment or the employer will usually provide a checklist that needs to be used for a particular piece of equipment at the beginning of each day or shift.

Safety and maintenance checks will vary based on the type of equipment: whether it is manually- or machine-powered and the size and traffic volume of the equipment are factors that influence what checks must be performed.

Below is a sample checklist for a forklift operator. In larger companies, a maintenance crew rather than the equipment operator may perform some of these checks.

Chapter 5

Supply Chain Logistics

Safety and Operational Checks (Prior to each shift)
Have a qualified mechanic correct all problems

Engine Off Checks	OK	Maintenance
Leaks – Fuel, Hydraulic Oil, Engine Oil or Radiator Coolant		
Tires – Condition and Pressure		
Forks, Top Clip Retaining Pin and Heel – Check Condition		
Load Backrest – Securely Attached		
Hydraulic Hoses, Mast Chains, Cables and Stops – Check Visually		
Overhead Guard – Attached		
Finger Guards – Attached		
Propane Tank (LP Gas Truck) – Rust Corrosion, Damage		
Safety Warnings – Attached (Refer to Parts Manual for Location)		
Battery – Check Water/Electrolyte Level and Charge		
All Engine Belts – Check Visually		
Hydraulic Fluid Level – Check Level		
Engine Oil Level – Dipstick		
Transmission Fluid Level – Dipstick		
Engine Air Cleaner – Squeeze Rubber Dirt Trap or Check the Restriction Alarm (if equipped)		
Fuel Sedimentor (Diesel)		
Radiator Coolant – Check Level		
Operator's Manual – In Container		
Nameplate – Attached and Information Matches Model, Serial Number and Attachments		
Seat Belt – Functioning Smoothly		
Hood Latch – Adjusted and Securely Fastened		
Brake Fluid – Check Level		
Engine On Checks – Unusual Noises Must Be Investigated Immediately	OK	Maintenance
Accelerator or Direction Control Pedal – Functioning Smoothly		
Service Brake – Functioning Smoothly		
Parking Brake – Functioning Smoothly		
Steering Operation – Functioning Smoothly		
Drive Control – Forward/Reverse – Functioning Smoothly		
Tilt Control – Forward and Back – Functioning Smoothly		
Hoist and Lowering Control – Functioning Smoothly		
Attachment Control – Operation		
Horn and Lights – Functioning		
Cab (if equipped) – Heater, Defroster, Wipers – Functioning		
Gauges: Ammeter, Engine Oil Pressure, Hour Meter, Fuel Level, Temperature, Instrument Monitors – Functioning		

All operators must be trained and evaluated on the types of industrial trucks and attachments they will be operating.

Supply Chain Logistics

Notes

Supply Chain Logistics

Foundational Knowledge:
For Frontline Workers

Chapter 1:
Global Supply Chain Logistic

Chapter 2:
The Logistics Environment

Chapter 3:
Material Handling Equipment

Chapter 4:
Safety Principles

Chapter 5:
Safe Material Handling & Equipment Operation

Chapter 6:
Quality Control Principles

Chapter 7:
Work Communication

Chapter 8:
Teamwork & Good Workplace Conduct to Solve Problems

Chapter 9:
Using Computers

OVERVIEW OF CHAPTER

The purpose of this chapter is to explain the basic quality control principles and systems used in logistics. Quality Control is the practice of ensuring that the correct products arrive at the correct location at the correct time. This chapter will explain various methods companies use to measure and improve the quality of their systems and processes.

OBJECTIVES

When you have completed this chapter, you will be able to do these things.

1. **Identify** and characterize key quality control systems in a logistics environment
2. **Provide** examples of how frontline workers support these systems
3. **Provide** examples of how frontline workers support these systems
4. **Explain** quality audits and how frontline workers support them.
5. **Explain** how to present quality improvement recommendations to supervisors

Supply Chain Logistics

Chapter 6

Quality control in logistics means the right products, at the right time, in the right condition.

Every employee, from entry-level through upper management, plays a role in quality control.

Quality Control

What Is Quality?

The three basic quality objectives in the logistics environment are accurate, on-time and damage-free handling of materials. Quality control is the process used to ensure that products meet or exceed customer expectations and are delivered to the customer on-time and without damage.

Quality control needs to be assured in all four of the basic functions of any distribution center or warehouse: receiving, stocking, picking and shipping. These four major functions are directed by inventory control, which might be called the "quality control department" in logistics operations.

Workers in inventory control are normally very experienced employees who are familiar with all aspects of warehouse operation. They have in-depth knowledge of the computer systems that control the inventory as it moves through the warehouse.

Controlling & Improving Quality

Quality in the logistics arena is just as important as it is in the manufacturing process. The effort to constantly improve quality has been adopted by most major distribution facilities. Customers demand a high degree of quality and customer service to back it up.

Key Elements of Quality

Because of the financial impact that receiving errors can have on a company, quality in the logistics environment begins with the auditing function in the receiving process. If a receiving person signs for $100,000 and then finds that the order was $10,000 short, the company could be out the $10,000.

Supply Chain Logistics

Chapter 6

Companies that receive a large amount of expensive products will commonly station two or three auditors in this department.

Joseph Juran, a leading quality control expert, defined quality as fitness for use. His system is based on knowing what the customer wants. According to Juran, there are three elements that lead to reduced costs and improved production: planning, control and improvement.

Quality planning is designing a process that is capable of meeting quality standards. It begins with identifying the customer and determining what they need and want. The process includes developing controls to ensure that the final product or process continues to meet the company standards and the needs of the customer.

Quality Control. Some degree of statistical process control (SPC) can be used in regard to the order processing function. Pick accuracy is something that most distribution centers track on a consistent basis that lends itself to this kind of a process. It is relatively easy to keep track of where mistakes are being made and therefore adjust the auditing cycle to remedy the problem.

For quality control to be effective everyone involved in the process must have knowledge of how it works and of both external and internal customer needs. Since frontline workers are directly involved in day-to-day material handling, they are well positioned to recognize ways to improve quality control. They must be willing to make recommendations for improvement when the processes in which they are engaged may result in errors or defects.

Quality Improvement. Quality improvement means finding a better way of meeting customer needs. Teaming with human resources to identify training needs that eliminate errors is one of the things that can have significant impact on future quality results. One should work with all team members to develop new ideas for process improvements, including the use of new technologies.

Quality improvements may also be required when the customer's needs change. For example, some customers will accept "back orders" while other customers will not, some will accept substitutions while others will not, some will accept partial orders while others will not. All of these requirements must be followed to fulfill the customer's needs.

Quality & Cost

Implementing a quality program costs money. Costs include:

- Quality training for all employees
- Auditing at various stages of the order cycle
- Extensive documentation and record keeping, which require a commitment of time and resources

Companies are willing to incur these costs because the cost of having to do the work over and reship the product is much greater, not to mention the possibility of losing a customer. Picking and shipping errors cost warehouse and distribution centers a great deal of money every year.

Supply Chain Logistics

Chapter 6

Did You Know?

Lean Logistics

Lean and Six Sigma practices originated in the manufacturing industry, but the principles are still applicable to logistics and material handling. Companies apply lean principles to the logistics process by reducing inventory, reducing waste and reducing mistakes. The results are increased efficiency, lower costs, fewer errors and faster turnaround times.

Reducing Inventory. Keeping less inventory on hand is one way to apply lean principles to logistics operations. This may be accomplished through cross-docking and just-in-time delivery. Cross-docking means that a shipment arrives just-in-time to be sorted and placed on other outbound vehicles for transport with little or no storage time in between.

Reducing Waste. There are many ways to reduce waste in the logistics process. When considering waste reduction from a lean perspective, it is not always about reducing physical waste. Although that is certainly one aspect of lean. From a logistics point of view, waste reduction can mean anything from reducing the amount of travel time used by an order picker, to smaller package sizes that maximize container space and reduce transportation costs.

Reducing Mistakes. Since lean principles aim to increase efficiency, there is a requirement to produce more results, faster. However, that can lead to more mistakes. In order to make a process "mistake-proof", companies may introduce more technology driven solutions such as barcoding, RFID and voice recognition to speed up an order picking process but still maintain high accuracy.

If defects are not discovered until the product is delivered to the customer, costs also include:

- Additional shipping and handling costs to resend the products
- Warranty costs and liability issues
- Possible recall costs
- Most important, the potential loss of customer satisfaction and possible loss of future business

In the end, these costs can far outweigh the costs of preventing problems with a quality control program.[1]

Quality Control Systems

Improvement in quality is an ongoing responsibility of every employee in an organization from the front-line worker to the CEO. This section will introduce some of the most common quality control systems used today.

Lean

Lean is practice that seeks to eliminate waste. It focuses on increasing efficiency, decreasing waste, and using empirical methods to decide what matters, rather than uncritically accepting pre-existing ideas and ways of doing things. Lean is based on eliminating seven "muda" or wastes from the process:

- Transportation or movement that is unnecessary
- Inventory that is not being used (This principle is linked to Just-in-Time inventory management to reduce inventory.)
- Motion that is more than required to complete a task
- Waiting (periods of inactivity)

Supply Chain Logistics

Chapter 6

- Overproduction, including that which is ahead of demand
- Over processing
- Defects (including inspecting and repairing defects)

Employee Guidelines for Safer Lifting and Carrying

Six Sigma

Six Sigma is a business management strategy originally developed by Motorola. "It is a set of quality management tools that uses a statistical data approach to reduce defects and improve and maintain quality. The objective of Six Sigma is to use measurements to focus on process improvement and reduce variation. The Six Sigma strategy to improve quality is based on a series of systematic problem-solving steps known as DMAIC (Define, Measure, Analyze, Improve, and Control).

"To achieve Six Sigma, the process must produce no more than 3.4 defects per million opportunities. A defect is any variance that is outside the customer specifications. An opportunity is a chance for a defect to occur."[2]

Total Quality Management (TQM)

TQM is a system built around an effort to improve quality, to involve everyone in the organization and most importantly, to ensure customer satisfaction. A TQM approach "requires that the company find out what the customer wants, design the product to meet or exceed customer needs, and design the process to operate without the need for corrective action."[3] Data is a chief element in this system because it is used to track results. Another important element of TQM is continuous improvement. This concept is called kaizen, the Japanese term meaning "continuous improvement".

Supply Chain Logistics

Chapter 6

The objective of TQM is to provide a quality product to customers at a lower price. By increasing quality and decreasing price, profit and growth will increase, which will increase job security and employment."[4] This approach focuses on the whole supply chain, from beginning to end. It recognizes that customer satisfaction and ultimately profitability depend on quality processes throughout the life of a product.

The concepts of TQM are:[5]

- *Customer-focused.* This means providing the best possible product at the lowest possible price.

- *Committed senior management.* TQM focuses on a top-down approach. It is based on the belief that quality control is a part of an organization's culture, which is directed from management to front-line workers.

- *Continuous process improvement.* The TQM approach asks managers and workers to recognize that there is always room for improvement.

- *Total workforce.* Total quality management is the responsibility of everyone in the organization. It means training all personnel in the techniques of product and process improvement and creating a new culture. It means empowering people.

- *Partnering.* Focusing on working with suppliers instead of viewing the relationship as adversarial.

- *Performance measures.* Improvement is not possible unless there is some way to measure the results.

International Organization of Standardization (ISO)
Many quality management systems are designed to meet the requirements of the International Organization of Standardization (ISO). "ISO's goal is to promote

Supply Chain Logistics

Chapter 6

worldwide standards to improve operating efficiency and productivity and to reduce costs. ISO publishes the ISO 9000, a family of international standards that apply to the design and implementation of quality systems. Adherence to these standards is essential for most companies that sell products to the international market."[6] ISO 9000 is a quality management system of standards that applies to systems that produce products. ISO quality standards are based on eight quality management principles which are closely linked to TQM principles:[7]

- *Customer focus*. Meeting customer needs and exceeding customer expectations.

- *Leadership*. Quality systems only work if leadership is committed. Management must ensure that all employees understand the purpose of and adhere to standards.

- *Involvement of the workforce*. Every employee is involved. Everyone contributes to the quality of the product.

- *Continuous improvement*. Constant attention to opportunities to improve makes the company more competitive and flexible.

- *System approach to decision making*. Understanding that all of the processes are interrelated, and changes to one affect the whole system.

- *Factual approach to decision making*. Acknowledging that sound decisions must be based on analysis of factual data and information.

- *Mutually beneficial supplier relationships*. Positive working relationships with suppliers can reduce problems with materials used in production.

- *Process approach*. The system encompasses the entire process of product production and transport.

"The PDCA cycle is a simple process for implementing continuous improvement in four steps: plan, do, check and act."

Plan – First, identify the potential improvement and generate ideas to bring it about. Anticipate problems so that no cost are added through waste of labor, time and materials.

Do – Implement the change slowly on a smal scale to avoid major disruptions.

Check – Measure to find out whether the change has accomplished the objective. What to measure and how often should have been determined during the planning stage.

Act – If the small-scale change was effective, involve everyone in the process to review and Implement the change on a large scale. Then plan for the next change if necessary.

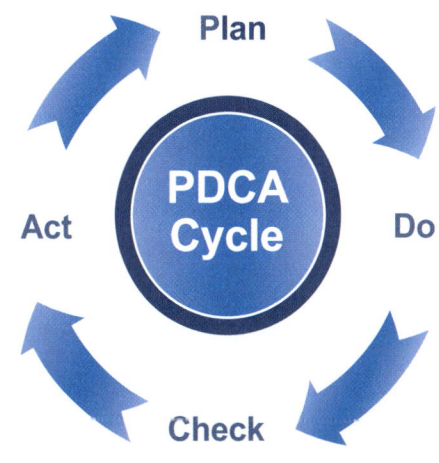

CLA: Foundational Knowledge: Chapter 6 - Quality Control Principles | Page 81

Supply Chain Logistics

Chapter 6

Front-line Workers and Quality Control

Role of Workers

Frontline workers in supply chain logistics are essential to the success of any quality control program. The continuous improvement principles previously discussed require direct input from the workers that are performing the material handling functions. In order to have a meaningful impact on the quality process, workers must be trained in the quality management system used by the company. They also need to be free to provide suggestions and ideas for improvement.

Their input becomes more effective when workers have an understanding of customer needs and demands.

Report Problems and Make Recommendations

What is an Audit?

A quality audit is the systematic examination of a quality system carried out by an independent reviewer. It is an important part of an organization's quality management and is a key element in ISO 9000. It is important that an independent reviewer conducts the review. Even though it is useful for workers and departments to review their own performance, that type of review is not the same as an audit.

"Someone not involved in the performance must conduct the audit to guarantee that it will be unbiased. For this reason, the worker responsible for the performance and the worker's immediate supervisor do not perform the quality audit. In a quality audit, an auditor is a trained, independent person or team that performs the review. An audit can range from a single part of a manufacturing process to an entire facility."[8]

Purpose of Quality Audits

The purpose of a quality audit is to provide assurance, through an independent review, that processes follow the guidelines of the quality plan and that the quality plan is adequately aligned with ISO standards. Essentially, an audit is used to detect problems and warn of potential problems before they develop. It is also a method to identify opportunities for improvement. Some of the objectives are to:

- Evaluate how well the quality system conforms to ts stated standards.
- Determine whether the quality system meets its objectives.
- Verify that the quality system continues to meet customer requirements.
- Identify opportunities for improvement and communicate those opportunities to appropriate personnel.
- Assure that products are safe and fit for use.
- Determine that Standard Operating Procedures (SOPs) are followed at all times.
- Ensure that front-line workers are knowledgeable about the process they are performing or monitoring.

Frontline workers are involved in audits in several ways. The auditors may observe them at work and may interview them to determine whether performance complies with standards. In addition, workers may be part of an internal, independent team that audits another company process that is outside their own jobs. In any case, frontline workers should know the quality system protocol for performing an audit.[9]

Supply Chain Logistics

Chapter 6

Types of Audits
There are three types of quality audits, depending on who requests the audit: internal, external and third-party audits.

Internal Audits
Someone within the company – a manager or quality team, usually requests an internal audit. It is conducted by someone within the company who is not directly involved with the process being audited. Internal audits are typically used to ensure that the quality system is being followed as designed. They can focus on a single process or product or the quality system itself.

Frontline workers participate in quality audits by answering questions, providing suggestions and being observed on the job.

External Audits
Someone outside the company – a customer or regulatory agency, requests an external audit. It can be performed by the organization requesting the audit or a third-party. External audits usually focus on processes of importance to the requestor, such as compliance with agency regulations or product quality.

Third-Party Audits
Third party audits in the logistics arena are usually associated with a physical inventory process. The company's auditing firm may send representatives into the plant to review inventory procedures and verify results of a physical inventory. Many large companies today use a process of "cycle counting" to avoid the difficulty of taking a complete physical inventory which in some cases means shutting down the operation for a day or two.

An audit may result in suggestions for process improvement or corrective actions.

CLA: Foundational Knowledge: Chapter 6 - Quality Control Principles | Page 83

Supply Chain Logistics

Chapter 6

Terms To Know

Audit
An objective comparison of actions to policies and plans.

External audit
An audit conducted by a third party (another company or department).

Internal audit
An audit conducted by someone from within the company or department.

Lean production
A philosophy of production that emphasizes that minimization of the amount of all the resources (including time) used in the various activities of the enterprise. It involves identifying and eliminating non-value-adding activities in design, production, supply chain management, and dealing with customers.

Non-conformity
Failure to fulfill a specified requirement.

Quality audit
A systematic, independent examination and review to determine whether quality activities and related results comply with planned arrangements and whether these arrangements are implemented effectively and are suitable to achieve the objectives.

Quality control
The process of measuring quality conformance by comparing the actual with a standard for the characteristic and acting on the difference.

A third-party audit is used to prove that the quality program meets a specific set of standards, such as ISO 9000. A team that has accreditation from the standards agency generally performs a third-party audit. A recent external audit that has been introduced into the logistics process is the Sarbanes/Oxley certification. This involves several security requirements along with some receiving procedures that must be followed to attain the certification.

Non-conforming Materials

Occasionally warehouse and distribution centers will receive goods that are later recalled by the manufacturer or are asked to put the product on hold until they can have someone inspect the product before it can be released for shipment. All warehouse and distribution centers have a process for doing this, which is normally controlled by the inventory control department.

Labeling and Segregating
Defective products may be labeled or tagged according to company policy. These tagged materials then need to be separated from materials that do meet quality standards. They may be placed in a labeled bin, container or section. A label or tag can be placed either on the container (for smaller items) or on the individual item (larger items) as it is segregated from conforming materials.

In some cases, the product may be repairable. Once it is repaired or brought up to standard, the label is removed and the item returned to regular stock. In some cases, the product is returned to the manufacturer or it is destroyed.

Supply Chain Logistics

Chapter 6

Documentation
It is very important that proper documentation is kept on any non-conforming or damaged product so that an audit trail can be followed in the event that a problem occurs in the future.

Terms To Know

Six Sigma
A methodology that furnishes tools for the improvement of business processes. The intent is to decrease process variation and improve product quality.

Total Quality Management (TQM)
A termed coined to describe Japanese-style management approaches to quality improvement. TQM is based on the participation of all members of an organization in improving processes, goods, services, and the culture in which they work.

Supply Chain Logistics

Notes

Supply Chain Logistics

Foundational Knowledge:
For Frontline Workers

Chapter 1:
Global Supply Chain Logistic

Chapter 2:
The Logistics Environment

Chapter 3:
Material Handling Equipment

Chapter 4:
Safety Principles

Chapter 5:
Safe Material Handling & Equipment Operation

Chapter 6:
Quality Control Principles

Chapter 7:
Work Communication

Chapter 8:
Teamwork & Good Workplace Conduct to Solve Problems

Chapter 9:
Using Computers

OVERVIEW OF CHAPTER

The purpose of this chapter is to explain effective communication within the logistics environment. Frontline workers communicate with various types of individuals from supervisors to customers. Knowing how to communicate effectively and professionally is an important part of any job. This chapter provides the tools needed for effective communication.

OBJECTIVES

When you have completed this chapter, you will be able to do these things.

1. **Explain** methods of effective communication between shifts.

2. **Explain** methods of effective communication to both internal and external customers.

3. **Identify** ways to elicit clear statements of customer requirements and specifications.

4. **Provide** examples of effective written communications in the workplace.

5. **Provide** examples of effective oral communications in the workplace.

Supply Chain Logistics

Chapter 7

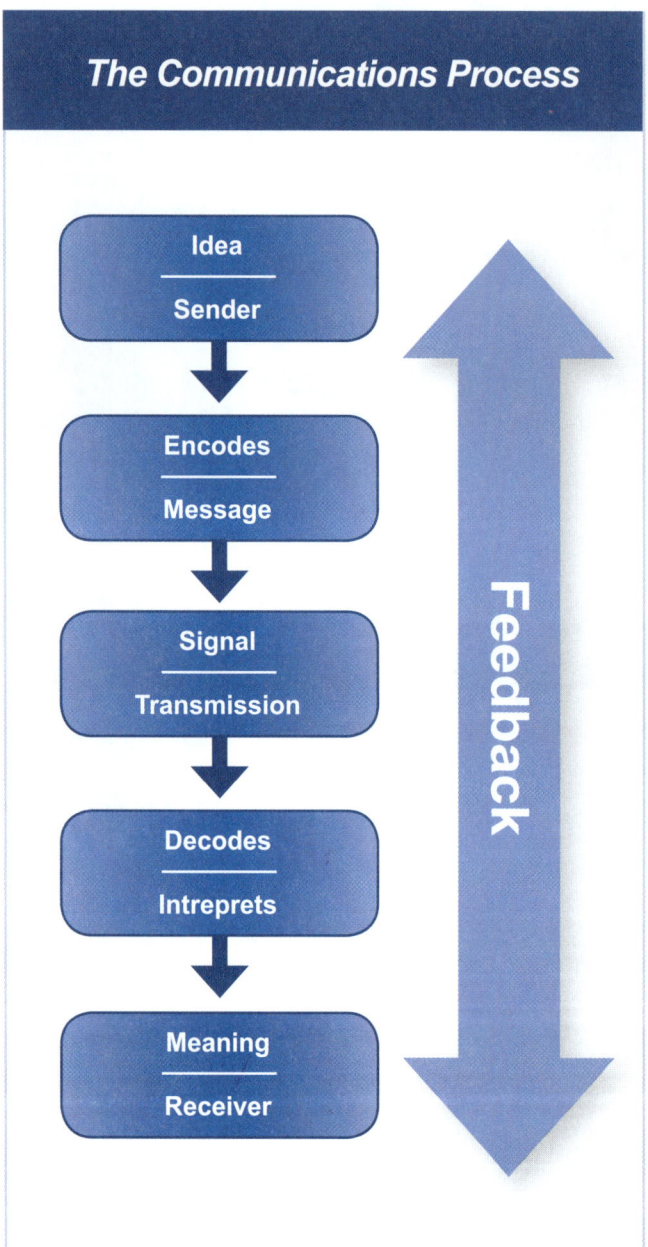

Effective Communication

Effective communication is a vital part of a successful supply chain. Within the logistics community there are two types of communication: internal and external. Internal communication includes that between workers, between shifts and between frontline workers and management. External communication includes contact with customers, vendors, suppliers, transporters, government or any other group outside the company. This chapter will cover general principles of effective communication and how to apply them.

Communication skills are essential for today's logistics worker. Most simply, communication is an exchange of information. One person speaks, writes or gestures and another person listens, reads or watches. In order for communication to be effective, information must be sent clearly and received with understanding.

The Costs of Miscommunication

"Most service failures in logistics can be attributed to breakdowns in communication"[1]. As mentioned in chapter one, supply chains are complex networks of suppliers, manufacturers, transporters and customers, each with their own requirements, guidelines and operations. Communicating effectively is critical to ensuring that correct products are delivered to the correct customer at the correct time.

Communication problems on the job can cost companies millions of dollars in lost time and materials. Miscommunication can cause delays, affect quality and leave customers dissatisfied. It also can cause tension between workers and make work extremely frustrating. Many communication problems are the result of what might seem like small mistakes, such as speaking too quickly, entering the wrong

Supply Chain Logistics

Chapter 7

delivery date or not listening to instructions. Each of these can lead to costly mistakes.

Speaking Skills

Oral communication is an important part of any job. Frontline logistics workers must effectively relay information to co-workers, superiors and customers. The following guidelines help to develop valuable speaking skills:[2]

- *Consider the audience*. Speaking to a fellow worker about a delivery is sometimes different than the way one speaks to a supervisor or customer about that delivery. Minimize use of industry jargon when speaking to external customers since everyone may not be familiar with certain industry terms.

- *Check for understanding*. Ask if the listener has any questions.

- *Speak clearly*. Do not speak too fast or mumble. Take time to pronounce each word. Speak loudly enough to be heard.

- *Use appropriate tone*. Some problems are more serious than others. When reporting a problem, make sure to convey the appropriate sense of urgency.

Writing Skills

The ability to communicate in writing helps one to find a job and perform it well. Frontline logistics workers use writing skills to communicate with co-workers and supervisors, generate delivery orders and report problems. The following principles will help make writing clear and effective:[3]

- *Identify the Purpose*. Is it to give information or instruction? To request information or action from a superior? To register a complaint?

- *Consider the Audience*. Just as in speaking, writing should be tailored to the needs of the reader. Communicate ideas to others in words and terms that will be familiar to them.

- *Clarity*. Use correct grammar, neat handwriting and simple direct statements to convey messages. When possible type or use a computer rather than hand writing messages.

- *Proofread*. Always double check for accuracy before sending a note or form. This is especially important with documents that contain order or delivery information.

Reading Skills

Reading is an active process. Whether reading work orders, equipment manuals or company memos, understand what was written and remember key points, especially when it comes to reading information on emergency procedures. The following strategies help comprehension:[4]

- *Preview*. Scan the document. Look at key headings and highlighted material. This will give a general idea what the document is about before beginning to read it.

- *Question*. While reading, think of questions about the material. This helps one to stay focused on the content.

- *Visualize*. Create a mental image of what is written. Visualize completing the steps of a described activity or completing an order correctly. This helps one remember it later.

- To improve understanding go back and re-read part or all of the material If necessary.

Supply Chain Logistics

Chapter 7

Whether listening in a meeting or talking to a supervisor, good communication skills are a vital asset to all logistics workers.

Listening Skills

Listening is also an active process. Hearing what others say and listening to what they say, are not the same. Listening implies understanding and responding to what was heard.

The following are some techniques that develop active listening skills:[5]

- Look at the speaker. Keeping eye contact with the speaker helps to maintain focus on the message.
- Ask questions if the message is not understood.
- Don't interrupt. Let the speaker complete a thought before interrupting with questions or opinions.
- Restate what the speaker has said in your own words. This helps ensure that the speaker's intended message was heard correctly. It also helps one to remember the important points of the conversation.

These principles of effective communication will be the foundation for the rest of this chapter.

Internal Communication

Excellent communication within a company requires effort at every level from the top down. Internal communication is that which occurs between workers within an organization.

Co-Workers

Most communication with co-workers will be informal sharing of information to keep each other up-to-date on daily activities. Listen attentively and give honest feedback to ensure that team members are able to function effectively.

Chapter 7

Supply Chain Logistics

Other Departments

In a logistics environment, communication with other departments is often needed to keep items moving through the supply chain. The department responsible for order picking must be able to effectively communicate with the shipping department and vice versa.

Other Shifts

Lack of communication between shifts is a common source of mistakes in the supply chain. Always communicate information such as which orders are complete or incomplete; what deliveries are arriving, delayed or departing; or any problems with equipment during the shift. This is an important element for both quality control and safety. Communication between shifts can be oral, such as telling an incoming shift of a delayed delivery, or written, such as filling out a checklist.

Maintenance / Repair Staff

Maintenance and repair staff are usually responsible for repairing and setting up equipment. Always explain any problems or malfunctions to help them identify and correct these issues.

Supervisors

It is important to effectively communicate with a supervisor. Whether it is a written status report or a conversation about a problem needing resolution, it is important to provide a supervisor with enough information to make an informed decision.[6]

External Communication

External communication refers to communication with anyone outside the company such as customers, drivers or service and repair teams. In some instances you may be the only contact a driver or customer has with the company. Clear, accurate and professional communication is an important factor in establishing solid relationships with these types of external customers.

Always remember to:

- Be respectful, courteous and professional
- Listen carefully
- Be direct and honest
- Ask questions for clarification or understanding

Communicating with Customers

One of the most important aspects of external communication is customer communication. Always ask appropriate questions and elicit correct information to process an order efficiently and effectively.

If there is a problem with a customer's order, call and speak with the customer and honestly explain the problem. When customers are communicated with clearly throughout the process of dealing with a problem they are more likely to be understanding about such a situation. Explain clearly what is wrong, the impact it may have on quality and delivery times and what the company is doing to solve the problem. Always present the company in a positive way. Do not assign blame to anyone or say anything that would make the company, a department or a team member look bad.[7]

Supply Chain Logistics

Chapter 7

Internal communication is between you and your co-workers, other departments and shifts and supervisors.

External communication is between you and people outside your company such as delivery drivers, customers and suppliers.

Modern technology has revolutionized the way companies communicate with their customers. "Electronic modes of communication have made order transmission virtually instantaneous."[8] The Internet and Electronic Data Interchange (EDI) have provided the ability for a customer's computer to communicate directly with a supplier's computer 24 hours a day, seven days a week. This electronic exchange of information helps eliminate human error and increase order accuracy.

Follow up with those who have been told that an answer or a clarification will be provided at a later time. Personal credibility is at stake. This is especially true when communicating outside the company.

Supply Chain Logistics

Foundational Knowledge:
For Frontline Workers

Chapter 1:
Global Supply Chain Logistic

Chapter 2:
The Logistics Environment

Chapter 3:
Material Handling Equipment

Chapter 4:
Safety Principles

Chapter 5:
Safe Material Handling & Equipment Operation

Chapter 6:
Quality Control Principles

Chapter 7:
Work Communication

Chapter 8:
Teamwork & Good Workplace Conduct to Solve Problems

Chapter 9:
Using Computers

OVERVIEW OF CHAPTER

The purpose of this chapter is to explain the importance of teamwork and problem solving in material handling. Being able to work together in a team is essential for a frontline material handling worker. Workers must arrive at work on time with a good attitude and the ability to work well with others. When conflicts do arise, workers should work together to resolve them.

OBJECTIVES

When you have completed this chapter, you will be able to do these things.

1. **Describe** a high-performance team.
2. **List** characteristics of an effective team member.
3. **Explain** ways to set team goals.
4. **Identify** use of team environment to solve problems and resolve conflict.
5. **Describe** typical requirements for good workplace conduct.

Supply Chain Logistics

Chapter 8

High-Performance Team

Definitions

A team is a group of people who work together toward a common goal, to complete a specific task within a specific time frame. Typically, a team will have three or more members. As a project continues, team members may find that they play more than one role.

A **high-performance team** emphasizes cooperation and collaboration among all workers to continuously improve company performance. "Cooperation is the key to success."[1] This is accomplished by sharing or integrating ideas, knowledge, skills, information, support, resources, responsibility and recognition.

There are different types of teams:

A work team is a group of workers responsible for similar process within supply chain logistics. It is vital to encourage cooperation between peers to establish good communication among operators.

A project team is a team that focuses on a single major issue of concern within a given process. Project team members typically take time from their normal responsibilities to work on a project team.

A cross-functional team is a team that is made up of individuals from different departments within a supply chain logistics facility or between facilities. For instance, a safety project team that deals with common safety or accuracy issues may be made up of individuals from receiving, storing, shipping and transportation. Cross-functional teams are typical in companies that run good supply chains.[2]

Supply Chain Logistics

Chapter 8

Any of these teams may be either managed or self-managed. A managed team is closely supervised by a manager. Although team members provide input into a decision, they do not make the final decision. As a team develops skills and delivers results, it may be given more authority for managing its own work. A self-managed team is a team that develops its own strategies, makes its own job assignments and monitors its own performance.[3]

Characteristics of a High-Performance Team

Defines Roles & Responsibilities Clearly

Teams often fail to meet a goal because team members lack clear roles. Team members may talk about roles and responsibilities in a meeting, but later they are not sure who is doing what. As a result, very little gets done and goals are not met. In some teams, the team leader assigns roles and responsibilities. In either case, high-performance teams meet regularly to update job assignments, assess programs towards defined goals and deal with unexpected problems. Team members may need to take on new assignments or help others meet a deadline.

Emphasizes Respect

High-performance teams try to prevent conflicts from arising by making sure that team members treat each other with respect. Some ground rules for that purpose:

- All ideas are encouraged.
- Differences of opinion are respected and explored.
- Key decisions are made by consensus.
- Criticism is always constructive.

Supply Chain Logistics

Chapter 8

Feedback can be presented in a formal performance review, or it may be more informal, such as a supervisor telling an employee they've done a good job.

In order for teams to be effective, team members must be properly trained.

Understands the Importance of Critical Feedback

The process of cooperation and collaboration within teams requires openness to critical feedback. The starting point is to understand and identify imperfections, and consequently, to encourage and embrace critical feedback from colleagues. This requires recognition that no team is perfect, that others may see the imperfections in our work more clearly than we do, and that critical feedback can be valuable in reaching team or company goals.

Acceptance of critical feedback applies as well to cross-functional teams. By focusing on a system-wide approach that diminishes silos, or functional barriers between different departments, an organization will make more effective decisions and positive results will grow exponentially. When this is accomplished, teamwork will thrive, costs will go down, revenues will grow and customers will be more satisfied.[4]

Understands the Importance of Training

A high-performance company understands the importance of effective, timely training. A productive, profitable and globally competitive company requires a front-line workforce with the current skills and knowledge needed for continuous improvement.

Training is provided primarily in three locations:

On-Site: On-site training is offered to incumbent workers at or near their place of work. This form of training can be offered by various providers, including company trainers or supervisors; vendors of specific processes or equipment; specialized consultants; technical college instructors who teach on site.

Supply Chain Logistics

Chapter 8

External: External training is offered to students, entry-level and incumbent workers at off-site locations such as colleges, high schools or for-profit training institutions.

Online: Individuals and companies are increasingly using online training technologies that can be used at any location where sufficient computer-based learning technologies are available—at work, at school or at home.

Understands Importance of Cross-training

Cross-training is the practice of preparing frontline material handling workers to work in multiple areas within their respective facility and where appropriate, within related facilities. Cross-training can improve a worker's ability to adapt to changing tasks, technologies and processes. Cross-training can reduce the overall staffing requirements.[5]

Characteristics of an Effective Team Member

Teamwork also can be rewarding for the individual worker. Workers who participate in teams tend to experience greater job satisfaction and improved self-esteem. Working in a team helps the following interpersonal skills:

- Problem solving
- Conflict resolution
- Persuasion
- Negotiation
- Cooperation
- Respect for others

Effective team members contribute to the team

Did You Know?

10 C's of Successful Teams

1. **Clear expectations.** Do all team members understand the purpose and goals of the team?

2. **Context.** Do team members understand the role of the team in the larger context of the organization? Do team members understand their own roles within the team?

3. **Commitment.** Do team members want to be on the team? Are they committed to achieving the goals of the team?

4. **Competence.** Does the team have all of the people and skills necessary to meet their goals?

5. **Control.** Does the team have the authority to carry out their goals? Do team members understand their boundaries?

6. **Collaboration.** Do all team members contribute?

7. **Communication.** Do team members communicate honestly and openly with each other?

8. **Creativity.** Are team members encouraged to share their opinions and ideas for continuous improvement?

9. **Consequences.** Do team members feel responsible for the actions of their team and accept the consequences of those actions?

10. **Coordination.** Does the team have a leader who helps them stay focused on the goals and duties of the team?

Source: Adapted from "12 Tips for Team building", Susan M. Heathfield, About.com Guide, August 28, 2013, http://humanresources.about.com/od/involvementteams/a/twelve_tip_team.htm

Supply Chain Logistics

Chapter 8

in a variety of ways. They have the characteristics cited below.

Contributes to Teambuilding

Building a team that really works well does not happen automatically. Working as a member of a team can be challenging, especially for those who usually work on their own. Those working alone tend to think of their own needs first. When working as a team member, the needs of the entire team take priority.

Each team member needs to play a part in building and sustaining the team. For example, they should work with other team members to:

- Determine team goals and related performance measures.
- Identify and discuss team activities to support those goals and measures.
- Prioritize assignments to match team goals.
- Identify tasks that will require a special team effort.
- Value each person's input into a team process.
- Listen to the training needs of co-workers who need to add their skill base.

Builds Trust

Team members need to feel that they can share ideas, ask for help and discuss problems without embarrassment. This requires trust. Trust takes a long time to build and a short time to shatter. Broken promises, favoritism, gossip and lies can quickly unravel a team. Follow these guidelines to build trust:

- *Communicate honestly.* Let the team know if there is an issue that may affect the team.
- *Communicate directly.* If a potential problem with another team member exists in resolving a team problem, speak directly with that person rather than talking to someone else about the person behind their back.
- *Keep promises.* Always make good on commitments.
- *Be fair.* Take on a fair share of the work and never overload one person or play favorites when making work assignments.

Helps Motivate the Team

The interaction between members of a baseball team during a game often shows team motivation. Team members encourage each other to excel. The same effect can happen with teams at work. To help keep the team motivated:

- *Be positive.* Rather than focusing on the problems the team faces, look for solutions.
- *Fix instead of blame.* Instead of condemning someone for a mistake, help the person understand what caused the problem and how to prevent it in the future.
- *Praise individual achievements.* Thank someone for a job well done. Share praise when the team contributes to the success.
- *Encourage team members.* A word of encouragement and a little help can make all the difference. When a team member is struggling, offer whatever support your skills and knowledge bring to the issue.

Supply Chain Logistics

Chapter 8

Focuses on Team Goals

Sometimes, a team can become too focused on day-to-day challenges and can lose sight of its goals. Effective team members should remember to ask whether the team is staying on track to achieve its larger goals. At team meetings, ask tough questions of yourself and the rest of the team:

- Is the focus on the team's priorities?
- Is more than is required being done in one area and not enough in another?
- Are customer needs the top priority when the team makes a decision?

In focusing on team goals, workers should also offer practical, achievable solutions. While high-performance teams respect contributions from all team members, those contributions should be informed and thoughtful. In making proposals for improvements, workers should do their homework, think through the implications of those suggestions and be practical.

Effective team members seek feedback about team performance from customers, managers, other shifts and anyone else affected by the team's work. Provide feedback on work performance that will maintain and improve performance. Resolve any performance issues in a positive manner to accomplish long-term production goals.

Supply Chain Logistics

Chapter 8

Ways to Set Team Goals

The beginning task of an effective team is to ensure that it has a clear, concise set of goals. Make sure everyone on the team understands exactly what the team is working to achieve. If even one or two members are not sure, team performance can suffer. One way to accomplish this is to use a goal-evaluation process known at "SMART." Each "Smart" goal is Specific, Measurable, Achievable, Relevant and Time based:

Specific. Make a general goal specific. The goal of "improving safety" can cover many issues. A goal of "reducing the number of work-related back injuries on the production line" is specific.

Measurable. Add a number or a percentage to provide a means of measuring progress. "Reducing the number of work-related back injuries on the production line by 50%" is a measurable goal. It is easier to measure than "reducing the number".

Achievable. A goal should be challenging but also achievable. When setting a goal, the team should be realistic about their skills and experience and the support they might need from outside the team. "Eliminating all work-related back injuries on the production line" is probably not an achievable goal. Reducing the number by 50% could likely be achieved.

Relevant. Make sure the goal relates to the company's overall business goals. If the company's mission is to reduce the number of work related injuries overall by 30% in two years, the team's goal should support that effort.

Time-Based. Make sure the team sets a realistic but challenging deadline for achieving its goals. "Reduce the number of work-related back injuries by 50% within two years." The team has a reasonable time in which to develop and implement strategies for achieving the goal.

Supply Chain Logistics

Chapter 8

Solving Problems and Resolving Conflicts

Solving Problems

As discussed above, companies are making increasing use of teams to improve performance. Teams are well suited to resolving specific problems. A team brings together more skills and knowledge than can typically be provided by a single worker to resolve complex issues. The activity of collaboration and cooperation can identify creative solutions and a common approach to applying them.

Teams can use the following seven steps to solve most problems:

1. *Define the problem.* Before a problem can be solved, it must be defined and the desired outcomes determined.

2. *Analyze the problem.* Before developing a strategy, the team needs to determine why the problem is occurring. Identifying the cause of the problem may involve interviewing people, analyzing data and observing people at work.

3. *Generate alternative solutions.* A team does not have to create an original solution to every problem. Perhaps a team member or someone else in the company has addressed a similar issue. Team members can learn from their experiences. Otherwise, they can research solutions on the Internet or in industry documents. Brainstorming can also be used to find solutions to a problem. Brainstorming is a process in which all members of a group spontaneously present as many ideas as possible. Everyone calls out ideas, creating a "storm" of ideas. One member of the team records the ideas which are not evaluated until all ideas have been presented.

Supply Chain Logistics

Chapter 8

At the end of the brainstorming session, the team evaluates each idea. In this uncritical atmosphere, people often think more freely and are more likely to present an unusual idea. Such an idea may be exactly what is required. If not, it may inspire another, more suitable idea.

4. *Choose the best solution*. The best solution is the one that will enable the team to achieve its goal while meeting time, budget and other criteria. Criteria are standards on which a decision may be based. For example, the solution must meet safety standards and be in place within a month. The team needs to examine the strengths and weaknesses of each alternative solution by asking the following questions:

- Will the solution help achieve our goal while meeting time and budget requirements?
- What are the risks and benefits of each alternative?
- Have others succeeded with any of the proposed solutions?

5. *Test the solution*. Implementation is the process of putting an idea into action. Team members may need to:

- Break down the activity into major steps.
- Create a schedule.
- Assign tasks to team members.

6. *Monitor and Evaluate*. Constant review and evaluation is needed when a new procedure is implemented. The team should meet regularly to monitor progress and make sure deadlines are met. If some part of the solution is not working, the team should be willing to change its strategy.

The evaluation of a project can provide some of the most important insights the team will gain. It can use these insights to improve future performance. During this step, the team needs to answer the following questions:

- Did we meet our goals? If not, how close did we come?
- Did we meet our deadline? If not, why not?
- What factors could be contributing to the problem?
- What other improvements could be made?
- What did we learn about our team's skills?
- Do we need to work on improving communication skills or building trust within the team?

If goals are not met with this solution, the team should go back to Step 3 and test the next alternative solution.

7. *Implement the Best Solution*. Once the team has found a solution that meets team goals. The solution should be implemented and monitored to ensure continued improvement.

Building Consensus

There are several ways that teams make decisions. A manager can decide; a team leader can decide; the team can go by a majority vote; or the team member with the most knowledge about the issue can decide. These methods can work, but each can leave some team members feeling that their concerns were ignored.

Chapter 8

Supply Chain Logistics

Another way to make decisions is by building consensus. Consensus is when most of the people directly involved reach an agreement. When a decision is reached by consensus, most team members accept the decision. They may not be completely satisfied, but they are committed to supporting it. Consensus decision making works because every team member has a voice.

Resolving Conflict

Any time people work together, there is a potential for conflict. Conflict is not the same as disagreement. Disagreements among team members should be expected and often help the team make effective decisions.

Conflict can arise in almost any situation, for any reason, throughout the day. Conflict disrupts work and keeps a team from achieving its goals. Any conflict that does arise between team members must be resolved so that the team can get on with its work.

Conflict resolution is a strategy for settling disputes and solving problems between people in a way that is fair to everyone. The goal is to find a permanent solution to the specific conflict or type of conflict.

This strategy requires honest communication and quite often, compromise. The parties involved should meet away from other people at a place and time that are comfortable and non-threatening for all parties. Do not meet when feeling angry. The following initial steps for conflict resolution help ensure that neither party will walk away from the situation with negative feelings:

- Each party should describe the problem in a positive, uncritical and respectful way. They should not get sidetracked by unrelated or past issues.

Think About It!

Conflict Resolution Scenario

THE CONFLICT:

Sally, a purchasing manager, is a fast-talker and skims over details. She has just resolved a crisis that took several hours (and is exhausted from the effort). Tom, one of her suppliers, is a slower-paced talker who calls her to confirm the particulars on a proposal. Sally feels pressured to make up for her lost morning. Tom, wanting to thoroughly understand what he will be bidding on, thinks there is ambiguity. Based on their previous interactions, Sally knows she needs to slow down how fast she talks to lessen their frustration.

Tom feels she is patronizing him, even when Sally speaks slowly. He becomes defensive and stubborn, and his voice tone reflects that. She hears his defensiveness and that fuels her defensiveness.

THE RESOLUTION:

Sally should ask Tom if they can postpone the conversation. That should give Tom knowledge that her impatience will be more prevalent if they talk now.

If Tom needs to get his questions answered immediately, they need to be aware of each other's schedules, stress levels and reactions.

Tom needs to disregard Sally's tone of voice and focus on the words she says. He also needs to focus on the most important questions, even if it means he won't ask every single question. Sally needs to realize Tom's attention to details is part of his personality, and his frustration will increase if he doesn't get his questions answered.

Source: "Steps to resolve workplace conflict," Shari Frisinger, Reliable Plant, August 28, 2013, http://www.reliableplant.com/Read/16396/steps-to-resolve-workplace-conflicts

Supply Chain Logistics

Chapter 8

- Each party should suggest a possible solution to the problem that will be beneficial and satisfying to all. Resolving a conflict does not mean that one side wins and one side loses.
- Each party should evaluate the suggestion and explain which part they can agree on and which part is not acceptable.

At this stage, a compromise agreement may be possible—in other words, each party may be willing to give up some part of the solution in order to resolve the conflict.

If compromise is not possible, try to find a new solution. Begin by re-evaluating the situation and re-examining basic questions such as the following:

- Why is this happening?
- What exactly do I want this conflict to accomplish?
- What can I do to keep this conflict from escalating?
- How can I figure out and respect the other person's position?
- How will that help me solve this problem?
- How can I get the other person to meet me halfway?
- How will I deal with this situation if the conflict cannot be resolved?

By answering these questions, the conflict should be easier to manage and more likely to be resolved to the satisfaction of all parties.

If a solution is still not found, seek mediation—a neutral third party to listen and make suggestions for solving the problem. Another alternative is arbitration. In this case, the third party makes the final decision about how to resolve the problem. Both parties must agree at the beginning to follow the arbitrator's decision.[6]

Typical Requirements for Good Workplace Conduct

All companies set standards for good workplace behavior. This is necessary both to protect company personnel and property and to enhance company performance and competitiveness. Companies also set behavioral standards to ensure a pleasant, safe and productive work atmosphere for all employees.

All front-line workers in supply chain logistics should be thoroughly familiar with and adhere to these policies in their respective places of work. Companies define those standards in their Employee Handbooks or in published Codes of Conduct.

If an employee's performance, attendance or conduct falls below standard, it is necessary to consider the facts and circumstances of the individual case to determine what action is warranted. Generally, in the case of a minor violation of rules, workers may be spoken to and receive a verbal warning. Continued violation or continued performance deficiency may result in further disciplinary action, such as a written warning, or depending on the seriousness of the situation, in dismissal. In most cases, a progressive system of discipline is utilized to provide ample opportunity to constructively correct any issues.

When misconduct is of a serious nature, a worker may expect discipline, up to immediate discharge without warning. Examples of serious misconduct include:

- Violation of the company substance abuse policy including, drinking or drunkenness at work.
- Dishonesty and theft.
- Misuse of company funds.

Chapter 8
Supply Chain Logistics

- Failure to report to and remain at work and/or unexcused absences.
- Fighting, threatening, coercing or interfering with fellow employees.
- Harassing fellow employees, including sexual harassment.
- Sleeping on the job.
- Neglect of duty.
- Insubordination/disregard of supervisor's instructions.
- Immoral conduct or indecency while at work.
- Gambling on company property.
- Falsification of company records.
- Willful destruction of company property, tools and equipment.
- Unauthorized disclosure of confidential information.
- Permitting unauthorized personnel on company premises without specific permission by management.
- Violation of the company electronic communications policy, including protection of company information technology systems.
- Soliciting for any cause on company premises during an employee's working time or distributing literature to as to interfere with work.
- Possession of a gun or any type of weapons on company property or in a company owned/leased vehicle.
- Profane language, abusive, threatening or intimidating conduct towards fellow employees, management or customers.
- Any violation of the policy prohibiting unauthorized use of photographic, cell phone, audio and other recording equipment.

Why are soft skills important?

"Apparently 'showing up when you're supposed to' is considered a skill, and one that's actually somewhat hard to find, even when unemployment is so widespread," Allison Linn, CNBC, August 15, 2011

The most important skills for new hires include: work ethic, teamwork, punctuality and basic math according to a study funded by the Rhode Island Governor's Workforce Board, 2007.

"To be perfectly honest . . . we have a hard time finding people who can pass the drug test," according to one employer. Applicants were often so under-qualified that simply finding someone who could properly answer the telephone was sometimes a challenge.

"In the Manpower Group's 2012 Talent Shortage Survey, nearly 20% of employers cited a lack of soft skills as a key reason they couldn't hire needed employees. 'Interpersonal skills and enthusiasm/motivation' were among the most commonly identified soft skills that employers found lacking."

Source: "S"600,000 manufacturing jobs go unfilled due to applicants lack of 'soft skills'," Rick Moran, American Thinker, October 1, 2012 http://www.americanthinker.com/blog/2012/10/600000_manufacturing_jobs_go_unfilled_due_to_applicants_lack_of_soft_skills.html#ixzz2dHvux72R

Supply Chain Logistics

Chapter 8

Terms To Know

Cross-functional team
A set of individuals from various departments assigned to a specific task such as implementing new computer software.

Cross-training
Providing training or experience in several different areas (e.g. training an employee on several machines). Cross-training provides backup workers in case the primary operator is not available.

Project team
An inclusive term incorporating the workers assigned to the project, the project managers, and sometimes the project sponsor.

Work teams
Teams of employees formed to shepherd a particular work area or function.

In addition to company-wide standards such as those listed above, companies may also have additional, more specialized behavioral requirements related to specific facilities. For example, additional prohibited behavior for a warehouse/distribution center or transportation facility may include the following:

- Falsification of company records, including receiving and shipping documents, driver logs.

- Operating company loading/unloading equipment or vehicles in a reckless or unsafe manner and disregarding proper safety practices.

- Permitting unauthorized riders in trucks, forklifts or other vehicles.

- Making unnecessary stops and/or using company time or equipment for personal business.

- Using indirect routes and/or proceeding outside of delivery territory as listed on the manifest without authorization.

- Failure to immediately report all vehicle accidents, thefts and/or damages regardless of fault or extent of injury or property damage.

- Failure to properly secure delivery vehicles by removing keys from ignition and locking truck.

- Failure to maintain a valid commercial driver's license, if one is essential to perform the job.

- Failure to notify supervisors of returned goods orders or major customer complaints.

Supply Chain Logistics

Foundational Knowledge:
For Frontline Workers

Chapter 1:
Global Supply Chain Logistic

Chapter 2:
The Logistics Environment

Chapter 3:
Material Handling Equipment

Chapter 4:
Safety Principles

Chapter 5:
Safe Material Handling & Equipment Operation

Chapter 6:
Quality Control Principles

Chapter 7:
Work Communication

Chapter 8:
Teamwork & Good Workplace Conduct to Solve Problems

Chapter 9:
Using Computers

OVERVIEW OF CHAPTER

The purpose of this chapter is to explain how computers and computer systems are used in logistics. Frontline material handling workers need to have a basic knowledge of computers and the systems used to manage the logistics process. Whether it is a basic company email system or a complex warehouse management system, computers are used every day in logistics.

OBJECTIVES

When you have completed this chapter, you will be able to do these things.

1. **Identify** commonly used computer systems and software applications in logistics.

2. **Explain** main uses of computer systems by frontline workers.

3. **Identify** commonly used software systems.

4. **Explain** main uses of software systems by frontline workers.

5. **Identify** technologies used to capture and store logistics information

Supply Chain Logistics

Chapter 9

Web-based Logistics Solutions

- Online response to customer inquires
- Forecast sharing
- Inventory auctions
- E-procurement
- Shipment bidding, booking and tracking
- Online freight payment
- Warehouse application service providers

Modern logistics relies on computers to manage orders, inventory and personnel.

Computer Systems

The computer plays an important role in the logistics environment. The volume of data processed on a daily basis in any given supply chain makes manual data handling a costly and tedious process. Most companies need to keep track of thousands of components in a world of changing demand, supply and capacity. Even though most frontline workers will not use computers as much or in the same way as a typical office worker, basic computer skills are an absolute necessity for success.

Internet

The Internet is a connection of millions of computers around the world. It allows for the exchange of large amounts of information. The most common use of the Internet in logistics involves purchasing and transportation. Typical applications include checking price quotes, claims management, and pickup and delivery operations.[1] For example, freight carriers can carry wireless handheld computers which give customers the ability to track deliveries and can alert drivers of shipment errors before they occur.

Quite often, companies restrict the use of computers to company programs only. In fact, most frontline workers do not have routine access to computers. although most companies do provide an area where employees have access to computers for purposes of looking up benefits and other types of company-related information. They may also use computers in a somewhat controlled environment for training purposes. On the other hand, computer use by all employees is becoming more and more prevalent in the work place, and it is likely this trend will continue.

Supply Chain Logistics

Chapter 9

There are certain groups within the logistics environment that have access to a wider range of computer programs including internet. These are most commonly the inventory control department, shipping and receiving clerks, warehouse supervisors and other selected individuals.

Email
Electronic mail (email) is the most frequently used application on the Internet. There are many different email programs including web-based and computer-based modules, but the basic premise is the same: you type a message and send it electronically. Email addresses follow a common format: [User Name]@[Domain Name].[Type of Institution]. The user name is usually assigned by the user or the company for whom the user works. A domain name is the registered name by which an organization is recognized on the Internet. This can be a company name such as Valdor or Microsoft, or it can be a computer hosted provider name such as Yahoo or Gmail. The type of institution determines the suffix of an email address, whether it is a dot com (.com), dot net (.net), dot org (.org), dot gov (.gov), etc. For example, a typical email address might be: JohnDoe@yahoo.com.

Word-processing
This is a computer application used for composing, editing, formatting and printing a document. Microsoft Word is the most popular word processing application on the market today.

Spreadsheet
Spreadsheets are computer applications that simulate paper worksheets. They are grids of columns and rows which form cells. Each cell contains a specific piece of data that can be manipulated and calculated with other cells in the same sheet.

Microsoft Excel is a commonly used spreadsheet application. Spreadsheets may be printed and used by logistics workers to analyze operations, show inventory status or indicate transport modes.

Software Systems

Throughout the supply chain, various software programs are used to assist workers and transmit information. The following systems are the most likely to be used by frontline workers in a logistics environment.

Inventory Management Systems
The most widely used systems in the warehouse operation are Inventory Control Systems. While these systems are mostly used by the inventory control department, they are also widely used by front line workers. This program is generally referred to as WMS (Warehouse Management System) and allows employees to input a variety of inventory information such as quantity, location, status and other relevant data. Information is entered into the system when the product is received and then used to track the item.

Supply Chain Logistics

Chapter 9

Logistics workers may use computers for various applications on the job.

Instead of manually entering the information, modern technology has provided the ability to scan items directly into the system using barcodes or RFID tags, which will be explained later in this chapter. Most interaction with inventory control systems will be done through hand-held devices which capture inventory information as it is entering, leaving or moving through a facility. The primary purpose of a WMS is to control the movement and storage of materials within a warehouse. The system processes transactions associated with shipping, receiving, storing and picking.

Other Software Programs
A Customer Response / Customer Relations

Customer Relations Management (CRM) software is used by companies to handle contact with customers. It stores such information as: customer contacts, communication tracking and order history. Employees can enter and access information. Front-line workers and first-line supervisors may need to use CRMs to access customer data if there is a problem with a delivery or order, but usually these programs are only used by customer service departments.

Transportation Management Systems (TMS)

A TMS is a software system designed to manage transportation operations. The basic functions of a TMS are: planning and optimizing transport, mode and carrier selection, real-time vehicle tracking, vehicle load and route optimization, load cost estimation, order batching and key performance indicators and statistics for carriers.

Supply Chain Logistics

Chapter 9

Capturing Logistics Information

Most errors in logistics records are caused by human entry error. Automating data entry and retrieval processes is one way to reduce these errors. Most logistic software systems are designed to integrate automatic identification technologies meaning that information is captured and transmitted into the system simultaneously.

Bar Codes

A bar code system includes a bar code representation and a scanner which can read that code. The most common bar code symbol is the Universal Product Code (UPC). Bar code scanners read bar codes by either direct contact or relatively close range infrared or laser scanners. Bar codes are used for a variety of identification purposes in logistics including products, containers, locations, equipment and documents. Bar code systems are relatively inexpensive and easy to use making it one of the most common automated data retrieval systems in use.

Radio Frequency Identification (RFID)

RFID works in a way similar to bar codes, but rather than light it uses reflected radio waves from a small device or tag to receive its information.[2] RFID uses an electronic product code (EPC) or similar numbering system. The EPC is universal to all EPC-compliant systems and determines how the data stored on the tag is read and used by the system. This ensures that RFID tags can be read by different scanners throughout the supply chain.

Barcode scanners are a common data collection tool that receives input from barcodes and transmits it to a WMS.

Supply Chain Logistics

Chapter 9

Terms To Know

Bar code
A series of alternating bars and spaces printed or stamped on parts, containers, labels, or other media, representing encoded information that can be read by electronic readers. A bar code is used to facilitate timely and accurate input of data to a computer system.

Customer relationship management (CRM)
A marketing philosophy based on putting the customer first. The collection and analysis of information designed for sales and marketing decision support (as contrasted to enterprise resources planning information) to understand and support existing and potential customer needs. It includes account management, catalog and order entry, payment processing, credits and adjustments, and other functions.

Radio frequency identification (RFID)
A system using electronic tags to store data about items. Accessing these data is accomplished through a specific radio frequency and does not require close proximity or line-of-sight access for data retrieval.

While RFID is more expensive than bar coding, it provides some significant advantages. RFID does not require direct contact or line of sight; it can provide real-time, in-transit tracking, and it can be used as a security and/or information device. RFID allows companies to know how much inventory is in the warehouse, how much is on its way to distribution centers and stores and how much is currently on the shelves at a retail outlet.

Other Systems

Bar codes and RFID tags are the most common automated identification systems in use in today's supply chain because of their practicality and low cost. But there are two additional systems that are used in certain instances: magnetic stripes and optical recognition devices.

Magnetic Stripe

Magnetic stripes (mag stripes) are the strips you see on the back of a credit or ATM card. The magnetic stripe contains an encoded identification number that is preprogrammed and cannot be changed without reprogramming the card. The stripe can only be read through direct contact with the reader, and can be accidentally erased by coming in contact with another card or a strong magnetic field. They are also more expensive than bar coding and RFID. In the logistics environment, mag stripes are most commonly used on ID cards for personnel for security or identification purposes. For example, an employee might use a smart card to gain entry to a facility, or a driver may carry a card which contains trailer load information.

Chapter 9: Supply Chain Logistics

Optical Systems

Optical or visual systems use cameras to capture information which is interpreted by computers. The most popular use optical character recognition (OCR) is by the U.S. Postal Service. OCR readers scan handwritten zip codes and translate the information into a bar code that will be used from that point forward.

Terms To Know

Transportation management system (TMS)
A computerized system to manage the operation of transportation systems including deciding on modes of transportation, planning imports and exports, planning and controlling fleet service activities, and load planning and optimization.

Warehouse management system (WMS)
A system that manages all processes that a warehouse carries out. These processes include receiving, picking, and shipping.

Supply Chain Logistics

Glossary

Accident
An event causing injury, ill-health or property damage.

Audit
An objective comparison of actions to policies and plans.

Automated Guided Vehicle (AGV) System
A transportation network that automatically routes one or more material handling devices, such as carts or pallet trucks, and positions them at predetermined destinations without operator intervention.

Bar code
A series of alternating bars and spaces printed or stamped on parts, containers, labels, or other media, representing encoded information that can be read by electronic readers. A bar code is used to facilitate timely and accurate input of data to a computer system.

Container Security Initiative (CSI)
A program of the U.S. government which seeks to ensure that containers entering the country's ports are scanned and deemed safe before departing their country of origin.

Corrective maintenance
The maintenance required to restore an item to a satisfactory condition.

Counterbalance
When the weight of a lift truck offsets the weight of the load it carries.

Cross-docking
The process of moving items directly from an incoming trailer or container to an outgoing trailer or container with little or no storage time in between.

Cross-functional team
A set of individuals from various departments assigned to a specific task such as implementing new computer software.

Cross-training
Providing training or experience in several different areas (e.g. training an employee on several machines). Cross-training provides backup workers in case the primary operator is not available.

Customer relationship management (CRM)
A marketing philosophy based on putting the customer first. The collection and analysis of information designed for sales and marketing decision support (as contrasted to enterprise resources planning information) to understand and support existing and potential customer needs. It includes account management, catalog and order entry, payment processing, credits and adjustments, and other functions.

Customs-Trade Partnership Against Terrorism (C-TPAT):
A voluntary system established by the U.S. Bureau of Customs and Border Protection with the primary goal of creating and environment of close cooperation between U.S. importers, carriers and international exporters to the United States.

Demand
A need for a particular product or component.

Distribution centers
A warehouse with finished goods and/or service items.

Dock board (dock plate)
A board or plate used to bridge the gap between a dock and trailer opening that allows people or equipment to move safely from one platform to another.

Supply Chain Logistics

Glossary

Ergonomics
Approach to job design that focuses on the interactions between human operator and such traditional environmental elements as atmospheric contaminants, heat light, sound, and all tools and equipment.

External audit
An audit conducted by a third party (another company or department).

Free and Secure Trade (FAST)
An agreement between the United States, Canada and Mexico which aims to speed transport of goods between countries while ensuring safety and security of the general population.

Grounding (electrical)
Connecting electrical equipment and wiring systems to the earth with a wire or other conductor to reduce the risk of serious electrical shock

Hazardous material (hazmat)
Any substance or material capable of posing and unreasonable treat to the health and/or safety of the general population.

Internal audit
An audit conducted by someone from within the company or department.

Job hazard analysis
A technique that focuses on job tasks as a way to identify hazards before they occur. It focuses on the relationship between the worker, the task, the tools, and the work environment.

Lean production
A philosophy of production that emphasizes that minimization of the amount of all the resources (including time) used in the various activities of the enterprise. It involves identifying and eliminating non-value-adding activities in design, production, supply chain management, and dealing with customers.

Material handling
The movement of items from one point to another inside a facility or between facilities.

Near miss
A safety incident in which an accident does not occur, but came close to occurring.

Non-conformity
Failure to fulfill a specified requirement.

Order processing
The activity required to administratively process a customer's order and make it ready for shipment or production.

Packaging
Materials surrounding an item to protect it from damage during transportation. The type of packaging influences the danger of such damage.

Personal Protective Equipment (PPE)
Equipment worn by workers to protect them from harm, including steel toed boots, gloves, goggles, ear plugs, etc.

Preventive maintenance:
The activities, including adjustments, replacements, and basic cleanliness, that forestall machine breakdowns. The purpose is to ensure that production quality is maintained and that delivery schedules are met. In addition, a machine that is well cared for will last longer and cause fewer problems.

Project team
An inclusive term incorporating the workers assigned to the project, the project managers, and sometimes the project sponsor.

Supply Chain Logistics

Glossary

Quality audit
A systematic, independent examination and review to determine whether quality activities and related results comply with planned arrangements and whether these arrangements are implemented effectively and are suitable to achieve the objectives.

Quality control
The process of measuring quality conformance by comparing the actual with a standard for the characteristic and acting on the difference.

Radio frequency identification (RFID)
A system using electronic tags to store data about items. Accessing these data is accomplished through a specific radio frequency and does not require close proximity or line-of-sight access for data retrieval.

Receiving
The function encompassing the physical receipt of material, the inspection of the shipment for conformance with the purchase order (quantity and damage), the identification and delivery to destination, and the preparation of receiving reports.

Recycle:
1) The reintroduction of partially processed product or carrier solvents from one operation or task into a previous operation. 2) A recirculation process.

Safety incident
An unplanned, undesired event that hinders completion of a task and may cause injury or other damage.

Six Sigma
A methodology that furnishes tools for the improvement of business processes. The intent is to decrease process variation and improve product quality.

SOP
Standard operating procedure.

Stock
1) Items in inventory. 2) Stored products or service parts ready for sale, as distinguished from stores, which are usually components or raw materials.

Supply
1) The quantity of goods available for sale. 2) The actual or planned replenishment of a product or component. The replenishment quantities are created in response to a demand for the product or component or in anticipation of such a demand.

Supply chain
The global network used to deliver products and services from raw materials to end customers through an engineered flow of information, physical distribution, and cash.

Total Quality Management (TQM)
A termed coined to describe Japanese-style management approaches to quality improvement. TQM is based on the participation of all members of an organization in improving processes, goods, services, and the culture in which they work.

Transportation management system (TMS)
A computerized system to manage the operation of transportation systems including deciding on modes of transportation, planning imports and exports, planning and controlling fleet service activities, and load planning and optimization.

Warehouse management system (WMS)
A system that manages all processes that a warehouse carries out. These processes include receiving, picking, and shipping.

Work teams
Teams of employees formed to shepherd a particular work area or function.

Supply Chain Logistics

Endnotes

Welcome
1. When Washington asked Nathaniel Green to serve as Quartermaster General, Green memorably characterized logistics as follows, "You mean the stuff that if you don't enough have of, the war will not be won as soon as".
2. Murphy, Jr., p. 10.
3. "U.S. Logistics Costs Hit Record High," David Blanchard, Industry Week, September 1, 2008
4. Frazelle, p. 2
5. Christopher, p. 4
6. Arnold, p. 10
7. "The Top 10 Hardest Jobs to Fill," John Rossheim, Monster.com Senior Contributing Writer, Oct. 30, 2008

Chapter 1
1. Hugos, p. 3 and Arnold, p. 5
2. Taylor, p. 21
3. Frazelle, p. 8
4. Howie, p. 1-7
5. Frazelle, p. 12
6. Arnold, p. 8
7. Taylor, p. 22-23
8. Frazelle, p. 224
9. Ibid, p. 229
10. Rushton, p. 258-9
11. Taylor, p. 23
12. Frazelle, p. 225
13. Tersine, p. 3
14. Frazelle, p. 42
15. Ibid, p. 50-51

Chapter 2
1. Rushton, p. 568
2. Ibid, p. 561
3. Stroh, p. 70
4. Rushton, p. 562
5. Melander, p. 5
6. Tompkins, p. 397
7. Arnold, p. 338

Chapter 3
1. Howie, p. 2:41
2. Ibid, p. 2:88
3. Tompkins, p. 495

Chapter 4
1. McGraw-Hill, p. 98
2. Ibid, p. 108-9

Chapter 5
1. Howard, p. 8
2. Ibid, p. 19-26
3. Tompkins, p. 896
4. McGraw-Hill, p. 103-5
5. Murphy, p. 129
6. Howie, p. 2:51
7. Ibid, p. 2:54
8. Ibid, p. 2:54
9. Ibid, p. 3:27

Chapter 6
1. McGraw-Hill, p. 352-4
2. Ibid
3. Ibid
4. Arnold, p. 468
5. Ibid
6. McGraw-Hill, p. 354
7. Ibid
8. Ibid, p. 377
9. Ibid, p. 378

Chapter 7
1. Goldsby, p. 94
2. McGraw-Hill, p. 132
3. Ibid
4. Ibid
5. Ibid, p. 130
6. Ibid
7. Ibid, p. 134-7
8. Ibid
9. Goldsby, p. 41

Chapter 8
1. Taylor, p. xv
2. Ibid, p. 16
3. McGraw-Hill, p. 145
4. Goldsby, p. 180-1
5. Frazelle, p. 272
6. McGraw-Hill, p. 152-6

Chapter 9
1. Murphy, p. 9
2. Arnold, p. 351

Supply Chain Logistics

Bibliography

APICS, The Association for Operations Management. APICS Dictionary, 12th Edition, APICS, Chicago, IL, 2008.

Arnold, J.R. Tony, Stephen N. Chapman, Lloyd M. Clive. Introduction to Materials Management, 6th Edition, Pearson Education, Upper Saddle River, NJ, 2008.

Barrett, Colin. Manager's Guide to Freight Loss and Damage Claims, 3rd Edition, Loft Press, Fort Valley, VA, 2003.

Cal/OSHA Consultation Service, Research and Education Unit, Division of Occupational Safety and Health, California Department of Industrial Relations. Ergonomic Guidelines for Manual Material Handling, CNA Insurance Companies, 2006. (Note: Document in public domain and may be freely copied or printed).

Christopher, Martin. Logistics and Supply Chain Management, 2nd Edition, Pearson Education, Harlow, England, 1998.

Colorado State Department of Transportation, Safe Operations Guide, 0900.01

Fergusson, Ian F. (9 May 2007). "The World Trade Organization: Background and Issues" (PDF) 2. Congressional Research Service.

Frazelle, Edward. H. Supply Chain Strategy, The Logistics of Supply Chain Management, McGraw-Hill, New York, 2002.

Goldsby, Thomas J. Lean Six Sigma Logistics: Strategic Development to Operational Success, J. Ross Publishing, Boca Raton, FL, 2005.

Howie, Allan. Fundamentals of Warehousing (An Introductory Course in Material Handling), Material Handling Industry of America, Charlotte, NC, 2003.

Hugos, Michael. Essentials of Supply Chain Management, 2nd Edition, John Wiley & Sons, Hoboken, NJ, 2006.

Long, Douglas. International Logistics, Global Supply Chain Management. Kluwer Academic Publishers, Norwell, MA, 2003.

Mangan, John. Global Logistics and Supply Chain Management, 9th Edition, Pearson Education, Upper Saddle River, NJ, 2008.

Manufacturing Skill Standards Council. High-Performance Manufacturing: Portable Production Skills, Glencoe McGraw-Hill, New York, 2006.

Mechler, Greg. Truckload Carrier Association's Daily Dispatch Challenge Training Guide. Delmar Cengage Learning, 2003.

BIBLIOGRAPHY continued

Melander, Paul. Hazmat Awareness Training Manual. Delmar Cengage Learning, 2004.

Mulcahy, David. Warehouse Distribution and Operations Handbook. McGraw-Hill, 1993.

Murphy, Paul R., Donald F. Wood. Contemporary Logistics, 9th Edition, Pearson, Upper Saddle River, NJ, 2008.

Rushton, Alan. The Handbook of Logistics and Distribution Management, 3rd Edition, Logistics Network, Dumont, NJ, 2006.

Stroh, Michael B. A Practical Guide to Transportation and Logistics, 3rd Edition, Logistics Network, Dumont, NJ, 2006.

Sweeney, Patrick, J., III. RFID for Dummies, Wiley Publishing, Hoboken, NJ, 2005.

Taylor, David. Supply Chains: A Manager's Guide, Addison-Wesley, Upper Saddle River, NJ, 2004.

Tersine, Richard J. Principles of Inventory and Materials Management, 4th Edition, Pearson Education, Upper Saddle River, NJ, 1994

Tompkins, James A., Jerry D. Smith. The Warehouse Management Handbook, 2nd Edition, Tompkins Press, Raleigh, NC, 1998.

Thompson, Julian. Lifeblood of War: Logistics in Armed Conflict, Brassey's, McLean, VA 1991.

Tuttle, William G. T., Jr. Defense Logistics for the 21st Century, Naval Institute Press, Annapolis, 2005.

Ward, Richard, John A White, Michael Ogle. The Essential of Material Handling: An Introduction to Equipment, Management, and Systems. Material Handling Industry of America, Charlotte, NC, 2006.

Weiss, Kenneth. Building an Import/Export Business, 4th Edition, Weilly , 2007.